THE *Black* SILHOUETTE

DENIECE "LADY" STORMER

Hardcover ISBN: 978-1-63616-023-8
Paperback ISBN: 978-1-63616-024-5
eBook ISBN: 978-1-63616-025-2

Published By Opportune Independent Publishing Co.
www. opportunepublishing.com

Printed in the United States of America
For permission requests, email the author with the subject line as "Attention: Permissions Coordinator" to the email address below:

Info@opportunepublishing.com
www. opportunepublishing.com

ROSES AND HOMAGE

Give me mines while I'm here too many times we find where people don't recognize how much they mean to us until they are no longer here to receive it and show gratitude for it. While I'm pretty sure that the people that have passed on appreciate the love, support and mourn that you do when they, or should I say when you, realize that you no longer can pick up the phone to call them, you no longer can write on their social media, you no longer can go to their house or even see them at functions.

This was probably my favorite part to write and the most important to me because I'm going to tell you right now if you love me, you better make sure I know you because once I transcend to the next dimension, I don't want to hear it. Especially when we are given resources and the opportunity to do so, so it's important to show love and appreciation to people when you can.

So, because of that, I took this specific section to take time and give some love and light to some people who have influenced me as a writer. I've had a lot of people in my life who have been influential and a part of me understanding myself as a writer and articulating myself as a writer. It pretty much started in fifth grade up to now, I have always taken a big interest in writing and understanding word usage, from enrichment writing in grammar school to the out of the box methods that my high school teacher would use to the expansion that my college professor brought out of me.

There have always been people who were placed in our lives to genuinely teach us even when they don't even realize it. My mentor has always been in my corner and always been there for me as guidance and listening ear. She is more like a big sister that tells you the ugly trust because she just wants what's best for you. She was very excited to hear that I was writing because she was one of the people who would, with no hesitation, correct you when you used improper grammar which helped me be able to articulate myself properly if I needed to or chose to.

It took two very special people to create me My father has always been an unapologetic voice to value when it counts the most.

My mother the best friend I never had there with me in the storm and frontline in trouble. Without you, I would not be who I am.

I want to take time to thank the light of my life, my grandmother, if you know me personally and if you don't know you will learn to know. My grandmother that is here with me on earth Carlotta is the center of my universe she is there with right or wrong good or bad, not caring or hearing what the world says because she knows my heart. This lady has always been an influence and supportive on anything I wanted to do in life, whether she agreed with her or not she's always been there, and for that, I am forever indebted to her literally

Some love and support you can't fake or buy, those who are truly there to see the greatness in you and push you all the way. I wanna thank my cousin, Shanita, my friends: Saaiba, Erica and Shanta and my friend Meme cousins, Precious and Shiann, my aunts, Tasha and Noody, my sisters and brothers and most of all my grandmother. These were all people who were there when I need opinions that were real and not scripted, they gave me some of the best feedback and automatically help me to create this piece of literature.

As we go through the world, we never realize how being who we are and building history can directly affects those who come across destiny. These people who may not have been close with me in the process but definitely weren't forgotten about because they have always been instrumental in my life and have at one point or another told me that I had a future in writing, my friends, Monica and Monique, my cousins, Nuk, Rhoda, Nandi, and my ryder, Gabby. While we may not speak every day I appreciate what you have done for me in the past as far as seeing something in me I didn't see in myself at the time. I remember plenty of conversations with each of you where you either laughed or just looked at me like I was crazy because I had one hell of an imagination and I can create a scenario out of just a few words. Those small things really impacted me in a big way and I just want to say thank you.

last certainly not least I want to thank God, the universe and my ancestors for my highest and greatest good, without this component of my life none of this would be possible I thank all of my ancestors that have transcended onto another life and keep their energy and love close to me. Continue to let your love and energy shine through as guide me through my journeys, none of you are forgotten and all of you are loved and missed. I sum this section up by simply saying thank you and continue to warm your loved one with your genuine love and support it may save somebody's life.

CONTENTS

The Black Silhouette That Flies Through the Day is a story about the insight, lives, history and thoughts of the characters who the story is based on. This story highlights the events and life lessons, demonstrating how they affect our lives as a whole and how we choose to live them, whether it be the decisions we make to the way we talk or even how we connect spiritually. Whether our actions and philosophies are conscious or aware to the point that we have an understanding of what comes with the territory or not, even the long-lasting impressions and morals can also affect us when we are unaware. There is no handbook or written code to life, and experiences can play a role, no matter your position in life.

During transitions, sometimes it is OK to shift your focus to learn what your purpose truly is. Obstacles and teachings are only small components along the way to finding your identity and understanding your life's purpose. While making decisions and creating your destiny, some things come full-circle and you end up back where you started. All you can do is laugh at the sense of humor that the higher power has while you go through life seeking a purpose that you may already be living out.

Everybody has their own fulfillment. Some people's lives can come together like a circle, while others' destinies travel in a straight line, where they seek out their goals due to trauma. As we all know, there is no perfect way to win the game of life—even the most perfect individual is flawed.

Despite all the teaching, experience and guidance in the world, self-identity and knowledge of self are things that you must find within yourself. The person who knows themself is more powerful than the person who seeks their sense of self from others. This person has no issue being able to use the gifts that they have developed because they understand their power. To be easily influenced and arrogant are traits of the weak and can ultimately put you in the mouth of a hungry beast who knows its power from soul to flesh. Soul ties are marked by the unmatched vibrations that one's touch can cause you to feel, making the hairs on you knuckles stand up; they come from passionate intimacy that takes over your body while feeding every erotic desire you possess. The danger in sex is the intent, the understanding that the person who you are giving full control of your body, mind and soul to have you at their mercy. These encounters can be deadly when the predator is inclined and knows their worth, but they can also be healing. So, hope that your intimate partners have positive intentions and that you don't end up on the losing end of the cycle. But have faith because you, too, have this power—you just don't know it.

CHAPTER 1
WHAT DO YOU DO?!

What do you do? What a classy woman! Fine as an automobile. When she walks, everybody holds still. Men hold their breath while the ladies grab their chests. Whispers of "Sexy as can be" travel through the air as the people try not to stare.

What do you do when sex is so good that you lose all control? You let everything go— your reserve, your words, your poise and your mind—because you want to believe that with a woman *this* fine, you should be able to leave life's problems behind.

What do you do when sex becomes your Kryptonite? Wrapping your mind around how what started out as one of the best encounters you ever had also became your last. When life's mistakes have seemed to look you in the eye, and your last moments are the prize? When excitement is tragic, and the only feeling you have is regret? Your soul no longer welcomes the joy and satisfaction of lust.

What do you do when it is time for a change, but you fight the idea of something different? Is it fear? Is it control? Who knows? Maybe it is the intuitive thought that it is too good to be true because you are who you are, and change complicates standards, but this is what you want because who you were does not matter and who you are becoming is the most attractive factor.

What do you do? How is it that the passion and love are there, and the breath on your neck sends shocks through your body, and your soul screams, "Please don't let this end"? This is soul-tying, unapologetic sex—yes, the thing you stay clear of because it has too much power.

What do you do? Well, you wear it! You endure the trauma while learning the lesson. You enjoy great sex and receive the tingles through your body when the memories cross your mind. You stand in your truth and welcome your diamonds while dodging your darts. You love yourself and realize that the fear of change is simply your higher self reminding you that there's more to life than what meets the eye and no one can rob you of what's for you—not even the old you.

CHAPTER 2
ASIA/ MAHOGANY MOMMY WIT' THE SLANTED EYES

Growing up in a middle-class, two-parent home, some things were just standard. For example, going to school and making something of yourself. Asia's father taught discipline, structure, balance and, most of all, stability. He was a handsome Black man with birth defects in his face that made the darkest room light up when he smiled. He had an outgoing and generous spirit, which gave him an advantage as a bank administrator. He knew how to talk to the people he worked with, as well as the customers, who were impressed by his knowledge of and passion for his work. He also was very predictable; you knew what he would do and what time he would do it. This was because he believed in the notion that repetition makes habits not second nature, but first nature because the habits then become a part of who you are when you practice them. This was one of many lessons that Asia's father taught her growing up. Asia's father loved her very much. He looked forward to her telling him stories to keep him up to date, and he loved hearing about her days because he would work long hours and miss most of them. "Tell me something I don't know, Pooh" is what he would say to Asia when he was ready to hear her stories. Accountability was an extremely big part of the learning process in their household. The children in the neighborhood tended to get their acts together when parents pulled out their belts—not Asia, though.

See, at a noticeably young age, Asia had a strange interest in pain and didn't mind inflicting it on others as well. She would play games such as hot hands, punch buggies and others that showed some type of pain or color change on the skin. This type of behavior flourished, making her a problem child and a target of violence at school. In junior high, Asia and four of her female classmates would walk around the school with name-plated belts. They would walk up to the boys and hit them with the belts. While the girls would never get caught hitting the boys with the belts or smacking their necks when they got fresh haircuts, the boys were no angels, either. The boys would grab the girls' breasts and run or squeeze their butts in line. These kids were bad and full of hormones. Asia's mother and father had to find creative ways to discipline her; in her case, whippings and beatings did not get the job done, so tactful methods such as involuntary work and taking of possessions were used. Even as a child, the idea of someone taking something that belonged to her just didn't sit right with her spirit, even if they paid for it. Asia's father would take the family out on vacation whenever he saw fit or whenever there was a need for a getaway. On one of their trips, her dad looked at her and said, "Pooh, this a nice little outing, isn't it?" Asia looked at her dad, squinting her eyes and blocking the light from the sun. "Yes, Dad, it is. The Earth is *so* beautiful, and nature is *so* relaxing and healing," she replied.

Her dad laughed and said, "Pooh, balance is key. You have to take a time-out to focus on you—the star player of your life—and those around you who give you unconditional and genuine love. Don't work yourself to death, but work hard enough to bring happiness and value to your life. Oh, and always follow your dreams, Pooh. Always follow your dreams." Unfortunately, that lesson was easier said than taught because he failed to follow his dreams. Asia's father was extremely spiritually gifted with his voice. He didn't have the loudest voice, nor did he project it the farthest, but there was something spiritually special about a man who could make instrumental sounds with his voice and cause people to desire freedom when he sang. His voice was so spiritually powerful that tremendous soul healing took place in many people by the end of each song he sang.

Stability was something that was drilled in Asia as a young child; she was taught that it was necessary to work for the things that she wanted and take care of others. There was always a need to care for people who couldn't take care of themselves, so she did just that. The fall after she graduated from high school, Asia decided that she would go into the Licensed Practical Nursing program at a junior college. In this program, Asia knew that she would gain the skill set she needed. So, she attended it. Asia completed an 18-month program in 14 months and graduated with Nursing Honors. Her teachers enjoyed having her in their classes and were honored to send her out into the world to help people. Her father was enormously proud. He deeply appreciated the fact that she took his lessons into consideration and applied them to her life in order to ensure her own success. She loved him and she loved giving him those bragging rights. She felt that he deserved them, so watching him enjoy them was the icing on the cake.

Asia's mother, on the other hand, was a different story. Her mother was the last surviving child of seven, which made her very lonely and caused her to become sheltered from the world. All of that would change when she was crossing a very busy street in the inner city. While driving his fancy car on what appeared to be a joyride with friends, a loudmouth with yellow skin and green eyes splashed a puddle of water into Asia's mother's face. He was a smooth-talking, younger version of her dad. Upon noticing that he had splashed the young woman, he quickly turned the corner to apologize for his negligence, almost hitting the curb.

"Hey, there, little lady. My apologies about that." Asia's mom wore a floral dress with coffee-colored pantyhose and black shoes. Her hair was pulled up into a top bun and her baby hairs were laid. "So, what's your name?" the man asked her.

"My name is Silvia," Asia's mom replied shyly.

"Well, my name is Juno, but everybody calls me 'Jews,'" the gentleman said.

"Well, hello, Juno. Next time, you should be more careful and considerate of others when you and your friends are riding around. There are people who still walk to their destinations and cross streets, you know."

"I am deeply apologetic," Juno pleaded.

"Sure, you are," Silvia replied.

"I am," Juno continued. "Let me make it up to you. Let me take you out."

Silvia looked at him. "I don't think so," she said. "I've seen you drive."

"It's nothing wrong with the way I drive. I'm a human; we make mistakes. Let me make it up to you, please."

After about three cute apologies, shy Silvia declined Juno's offer to take her out, but she did agree to allow him to call her whenever he wanted to talk. After a short period of dating, Juno and Silvia were newly married and had welcomed home their first and only child, baby Asia. Baby Asia was showered with love and affection from both of her parents from the day she was born. Silvia would walk around with Asia in the cuff of her soft, fuzzy robe, humming sweet melodies to her new bundle of joy while baby Asia rested cozily. On the other hand, Juno would make sure to be home at a decent hour to give his wife a break and have his bonding time with baby Asia as well. Like Silvia, he also would hold baby Asia in his arms; the major difference was that he would lay her on his bare chest, kiss her and talk to her about how much she was loved. About two years after Asia was born, her mother found out that she was carrying another child.

Shortly after, however, she suffered a tragic miscarriage that would prohibit her from carrying children ever again. Juno did what he could to console his wife and make her feel complete, but at times he felt defeated. That didn't stop him from trying, though. Juno loved everything about Silvia, from the scent of her perfume to the soft and feminine tone of her voice. They loved each other enough to get themselves through anything. Shortly after becoming a wife and mother, Silvia started a home business in which she created lingerie and other sexy clothing items. I know you're thinking that Asia had a front-row seat to the partying and sex that took place as a result of her mother making these clothes, but you couldn't be more wrong. She made clothes for the closeted freaks, the women who were a little more privileged when it came to their bodies. She made clothes for the working women of the neighborhood. Silvia's choice in clientele wasn't personal—these women simply happened to be attracted to her pieces.

Now, listen: She had nothing against women who partied or were promiscuous, as her best friend happened to be a dancer. However, she was not comfortable with having random women try on lingerie in her living room. Silvia was shy, not stupid. She was a chameleon who adapted to whoever and whatever she needed to in order to be successful. Silvia's most intriguing womanly and wifely trait was her ability to be soft and passive. She stood at five feet, five inches, which made her the average height, according to newspapers and magazines. She had rich, smooth cinnamon skin and dark, dreamy eyes that were slanted toward the left and right sides of her face. Down the center of her face was her cute button nose, and she had full, plump lips and fat cheeks with deep dimples. Silvia was a beautiful woman who wore her long, jet black hair down so that it flowed to her curvy butt. She moved effortlessly through the world with her iconic flat stomach, childbearing hips and perfectly sized breasts. Her physical features continuously turned heads, but she was a woman who restricted others' access to her body. She normally wore long dresses and four-inch heels, and she always did what she could to cover up her body with a long sweater on chilly days. Silvia believed that her body was for her man and for him *only*. So, the only thing the public would witness was her extremely submissive nature and intimate affection towards her beloved. She was extremely feminine and soft; she had a very welcoming soul and would use an understanding approach when dealing with people. Silvia was so warm that when Asia acted out, Silvia would shower her with love and understanding 'til she calmed down and submitted to whatever request initially caused the meltdown. This level of understanding was unreal. Silvia always seemed to have a positive outlook and she spoke life into everyone she came in contact with.

"Working late?" asked Silvia.

"Don't you do that, ma'am," Juno replied.

"I'm just asking a question."

"Well, my beautiful queen, I am going to join the bank investor at one of the local bars as a sign of gratitude for his generous contribution. He is visiting from out of town."

This was a conversation that took place on an afternoon while young Asia sat at the dinner table finishing her schoolwork. Juno grabbed a beer from the refrigerator and looked out the open window over the sink to see the neighborhood kids playing. Silvia wiped her hands with a kitchen towel, then walked up to her husband and hugged him tightly from behind.

"Silvia, don't do this," said Juno.

"I'm not doing anything; I'm just loving on my beloved," Silvia answered innocently.

"You're not gonna make this easy, are you?" Juno asked. "I wouldn't be me if I did," Silvia replied. "I'm just saying, we had such a good day. I didn't want it to end so fast. You should stay with us; enjoy dinner with your family."

Juno turned toward his clingy wife and agreed to stay. Silvia wrapped her arms around his neck and looked up at him with dreamy, puppylike eyes.

Juno sighed, kissed his wife on the lips and said, "OK. Nick got this. He'll be fine." He noticed a nosy Asia smiling and taking mental notes as her mom put the moves on her dad.

"Pooh, what are you smiling at? Your mother getting her way, as usual?"

"Yes," Asia responded in a giggly voice, smiling from ear to ear as her dad sat down and started tickling her.

Silva looked back at her husband and daughter as they laughed and played. She smirked and winked at Asia as their eyes locked, then turned back to the sink.

This was classic Silvia—using her loving and feminine nature to get others to submit to her. She never had to raise her voice; sometimes, she never even had to say anything. Silvia had the ability to give someone a look that immediately let them know they needed to get their act together. This was a look that Juno knew

16

oh too well, but he loved every bit of it.

While Silvia had nothing to worry about, she was a shy, timid little woman who struggled with depression and self-esteem issues. She was loving and nurturing. While dealing with life mentally and emotionally, she wanted to understand how destiny and spirituality worked. Although she didn't have all the answers and she had a lot of personal work to do, she tried to teach Asia the lessons that she had learned from her own mother.

Silvia would take baths and meditate in order to facilitate her thoughts and emotions. She would play meditative music and nature sounds and fill her bathroom with yellow, white and pink candles dressed in brown cinnamon, pink Himalayan salt, bay leaves, basil and olive oil. She would place white tea light candles around the rim of her bathtub, then fill the tub with water as hot as she could stand it. The bathwater would consist of lavender, bay leaves, basil, olive oil, sea salt, Himalayan salt, sunflowers, yellow and pink rose petals and a splash of Florida water.

The bath, candles and music, along with the intention to invite in positive and abundant energies was the perfect remedy that Silvia needed to get her through her dark moments. This self-care ritual ultimately became her go-to method to relax her mind and cleanse her soul. These baths and intimate moments with herself were very important to Silvia, and she made sure that they were important to Asia as well. When Asia was curious and mature enough to understand the importance of taking care of her soul, Silvia was extremely excited to share this lesson with her. Another lesson Silvia taught Asia was the importance of believing in herself. Silvia taught her all of these great spiritual things, which carried Asia through some tough times. The ability to feel, communicate and interact without words was so important. Silvia would set up different types of atmospheres and situations so that Asia could use her ability to feel in order to communicate and calm her spirit in moments of panic. Silvia would take Asia on trips to the park, bodies of water and even dark caves. These were tactful ways to teach Asia how to communicate with her body and not her words. Silvia would say, "Baby, it's OK to be smart and have knowledge, but if your soul ain't right or you don't have compassion, you would be just a smart, heartless fool."

"This is a cute lingerie piece," said a young worker as she walked through the store fixing and picking up clothes.

Another employee walked up to see what the hype was about. She looked at the piece of clothing in question and started laughing. "Yeah, for a dog," she commented. "My mother would have people lined up buying things in this store if her lingerie was here." Both young women returned to their stations behind the register.

The door swung open and in walked three young women between the ages of 19 and 21. One was a redheaded white girl; she had a real big booty and wore a blue jean romper with white tennis shoes. The next young woman was pretty, petite, chocolate Barbie who wore neon green pants, a pink shirt and black sandals with long bangs obscuring her face. The last of the three amigas was more natural-looking than the others; she was a thick girl and wore a red dress with red lipstick and sunglasses. Her hair was up in a bun and she wore bedazzled silver sandals. All three ladies had their makeup done and carried big Chanel bags to complement their attire. A younger, innocent Asia, wearing a black T-shirt and blue jeans with her hair pulled back, greeted them.

"Welcome to PBE, ladies! Feel free to look around. My name is Asia; please let me know if there is anything I can get you!"

"Thank you, ma'am! We will let you know if we need you," one of the three women replied.

Asia had just turned 21. She had decided, after spending two years in junior college and receiving her license as a Nurse Practitioner, that she no longer wanted to work in the direction she was headed toward. Even though she had changed her career and had no idea what she wanted to do next, she still needed to take care of herself—no one wants to fund the life of a grown woman who should be making close to, if not more than, $100,000 a year. So, she picked up a job at the neighborhood clothing store. She stood at the register, long-faced and deep in thought.

"What's wrong, Asia?" asked her coworker who was standing with her at the register.

"I do not know," Asia said. "I'm just thinking that I've gotta do *something*."

"Something like?"

"Something! Something that doesn't include me working a nine-to-five at a company I'm not completely invested in. I don't want to have to worry about training my replacement. I'm *definitely* not working here for the rest of my life."

One of the women who she had greeted earlier cleared her throat and called out in a loud, traveling voice. "Asia!"

"Coming," Asia responded. She approached the three women. "Hey, ladies, what can I do for you?" she asked. The women proceeded to tell Asia what outfits and sizes they needed her to check for in the back.

The young lady who wore the sunglasses recognized Asia and removed them.

"Asia!" she exclaimed. Asia looked at the woman and was shocked.

"Aw, man! Nicole! Hey! How you been?"

"I should have known that was you pouting at the register," Nicole said. "You've always been a big dreamer—if you got all the planets, you'd want the stars and the moon, too. Some things never change," she laughed.

Asia responded, "You know me—I want it all! And I was not pouting. I was just stating that I wanted something a *little* more exciting than this clothing store."

"Well, I ain't no entertainer who can guarantee you a billboard with your face on it, but I live pretty good, doing what I do." "I'm afraid to ask, but what do you do?" Asia asked.

"I'm an escort," Nicole answered.

"You mean, lady of leisure," Asia responded. She started walking toward the back of the store, laughing. Nicole stopped her. "Lady of leisure, lady in red, lady of the night, escort and every dog's best friend, minus the fleas," she said. Her two friends busted out laughing. "Fa real! Whatever they are calling it these days, I'm that! And no, I don't have some crazy, mentally disturbed, Cadillac-driving man taking my money, beating me up and telling me what to do. You know I do not even play with men like that." "Right, because I know you been gay since you were two," Asia said.

True, but I was born a freak, so this makes sense for me to do," Nicole said. "I come when I want, go when I want and do *who* I want. And I know you ain't talking about 'you afraid to ask.' If my memory serves me right, you were the Black Jesse Jameson and everybody knew, even my brother."

Asia laughed. "Well, I *am* talented, and your brother *was* cute." The ladies chuckled again. "Wait. I've never officially done anything like *that*," Asia continued. "I mean, it's different when you're, you know, getting paid, and I don't even know how to find people in the first place."

"That is why you should let me introduce you to my financial advisor; it's not like handing your money to a pimp. She looks for you when she needs you," Nicole explained.

"She?"

"Yes," Nicole replied, "her name is Blac. She fine as wine, but ain't nothing to play with. I am pretty sure that whatever you need to know, she got an answer for you. And as far as getting paid, that's even more of a reason to show up and show out! So, come talk to Blac. Let her bless your game and get you where you need to be so when she needs you, you can show up and get them coins or choose to stay at the clothing store."

Asia shook her head. "Girl, I gotta get these clothes." Asia walked to the back of the store, grabbed the ladies' outfits, and returned to the register. Nicole's two friends were already at the register purchasing accessories from Asia's co-worker.

As the ladies grabbed their bags, Nicole turned around to face Asia and said, "What's for you is for you. Don't sacrifice the goal because you're afraid of the journey. At least, that's what Blac would say." She turned around and exited the shop.

The other worker in the store walked up to Asia. "You know them?"

she asked.

"Yeah... one of them," Asia responded.

"I bet they strippers," her co-worker commented.

"No, they not strippers," said Asia.

"Well, if I was a stripper, I would make a lot of money."

"Girl, you ain't making nothing," Asia joked. She and her co-worker chuckled.

"Asia, tell me something," the co-worker requested.

"What, girl?"

"If you had a husband, would you dance for him?"

"What do you mean, 'dance for him'?"

"You know, pull out one of your mother's sexy lingerie pieces and dance," the co-worker explained.

"Ah, no,' Asia said.

"Why not? Plenty of wives do it."

"Oh, I know."

One night when Asia was 12 years old, she awoke and left her room to get some water. When she left the kitchen, she realized that a pretty blue light was shining in her parents' room. The door was not closed and the light brightened up the hallway. So, curious Asia walked very quietly towards her parents' room. She stood along the wall in a spot where they could not see her, but where she could see what was going on. She had never seen this light before and she was unsure what was happening. Asia was shocked at what she saw next. Her mother was dressed in all-white lingerie, along with a white mesh robe that was adorned with a white feather trim. Her mother also wore a headband that had white feathers around it as well. Her father sat in a chair in front of her mother, wearing only black silk pants.

On the small table next to him was a tall stack of money, along with a small cup filled with ice and a brown liquid resembling CocaCola. Now, Asia was never allowed to go into her parents' room, so seeing what was taking place inside was a shock to her. There was a long pole extending downward from the ceiling; her mother would grab onto it in order to keep her balance while she ran her hands through her hair and rubbed all over her body. Asia watched as her mother performed a sexy dance for her father in extremely high heels. Juno would stuff one-dollar bills into Silvia's lingerie, as well as throw them on the floor; Asia was shocked by what she saw. *First of all, why is dad throwing money at mom? Why won't he just put it in her hand? And why is she smiling and dancing and touching all over her body as if she's enjoying it?* Asia thought.

This confused Asia a lot, but she knew that her mother was happy by the look on her face, so she guessed it was OK. She watched as Juno stood up, grabbed Silvia by her waist and pulled her closer to him. He then wrapped one hand around her neck while biting her face somewhat gently and stuffing money into her bra with his other hand. Silvia's eyes rolled to the back of her head and she turned around, smiling as she looked into Juno's eyes. Juno grabbed Silvia by both of her hands and looked her up and down, shaking his head and sucking his teeth as if to say, "Damn, girl, you look *good*!" He let go of Silvia's hands, walked towards the door and shut it, not even noticing that young Asia was standing against the wall. Asia put her hands over her mouth. *I can't blow my cover. I'm not even supposed to be here*, she thought. Once she was certain the door was shut, she went back to bed.

Two days later, young Asia, after playing outside with friends, came into the house.

Her mother said, "Asia, I have to make a run up the street. I'll be back in two hours. Don't answer the phone and don't answer the door. Your father is working late, so he won't be home no time soon."

"Yes, ma'am," Asia replied. She kissed her mom goodbye and Silvia left to run her errand. Asia decided to watch videos and listen to music as loudly as she could, things that she was not able to do as freely when her parents were home. While dancing around the house and singing, Asia realized that her mom left one of her lingerie pieces out on the couch after trying it on. Now, Asia knew better than to touch her mother's merchandise, but for some reason, she could not get the recent image of her mother and father out of her head. She wondered if that was, as a woman, what you were supposed to do when you had a husband. So, Asia went into her bedroom and put on her mother's lingerie. She looked over at the feather boas that she and her mother would use during tea parties and wrapped one around her body. She looked in the mirror as she played a sexy '90s hit on her CD player and sang along. This was a very sexy song, and as she looked at herself in the mirror, Asia touched all over her body, just like she saw her mother do for her father.

Silvia burst into the room.

"What do you have on?" Silvia asked.

Startled, shocked and scared, Asia said nothing. She didn't know how to respond. Her mother repeated herself.

"I said, what do you have on? And I *know* that's not my good merchandise that somebody could possibly buy on your little 12-year-old body."

Asia, again, said nothing. She was afraid. She didn't know what to say. She didn't expect her mom to come back home so quickly. *That wasn't two hours*, she thought. *I just know that wasn't two hours. How?*

"I am not going to ask you again, young woman." her mother said. "What do you have on? Why are you dancing like that? Where did you learn that from?"

Asia looked her mom in the face and said, "I learned it from you." Silvia hoped she had misheard her daughter.

"Excuse me? You learned it from me? Why do you feel like you learned it from me?" Asia said nothing.

"Girl, I'm not 'bout to keep repeating myself. You said it; now, stand on it. Why do you feel like you learned it from me?" Asia nervously started to explain that she saw her mom dancing for her dad the other night. Silvia looked at her.

"I don't care if you saw God himself dancing or wearing that. If you don't take my merchandise off and put this room back in the way it's supposed to be and become the 12-year-old little girl that I left in this house before I left to run my errands, we are gonna have a problem. I'd better not *ever* catch you dancing or dressing like that *ever* again unless you are ready to accept what comes with that territory."

Asia responded, "Yes, ma'am," as her mother exited the room. She proceeded to take the lingerie off and rearrange her room in the way her mother had decorated it, but she just couldn't help but wonder why her mom was so upset. *What is the difference between doing what someone taught you to do versus what you saw them doing?* she asked herself. She remembered what her mother would tell her: "Do as I say, not as I do. Do what I tell you to do and do what I teach you to do. Don't do what you see me do because there's a reason why I do what I do. I can accept the consequences and what comes with what I do." Asia never forgot that lesson.

"Tonya, I panicked," said Silvia while she was on the phone with her sister, explaining what happened when she walked in on Asia.

Laughing, Tonya said, "I know you did if you raised your voice at little Ms. Perfect, even though she bad as hell!"

"Oh, you're one to talk," Silvia said. "How is the baby serial killer?"

"Stop calling my baby a serial killer."

"Stop it. You know I love Daddy."

"Me, too. I love my little Jason. But anyways, did you take the TV? Because you know that's where she learned it from," said Tonya.

Silvia said, "No, because according to my daughter, I could be a headliner at Magic City."

"I almost swallowed my teeth," Tonya gasped. "She saw you and Jews…?"

"Girl, yes," Sylvia responded. "It must've been the other night. I had a bottle of wine, and I was *done,* so we didn't close the door, and I guess her little nosy ass watched the show."

"And a show it was!" Tonya commented. "Then, you go yell at the baby? Poor Asia; she probably ain't have no understanding."

"I didn't mean to yell. It just kinda happened," Silvia explained.

"Well, it happened, so you can't take it back," Tonya explained. All you can do is have a conversation so that she knows where you were coming from. Now, I know you don't believe in that, but your response was out of love and fear, so the intent wasn't wrong. But the delivery was, so don't beat ya'self up."

"Yeah, I guess."

"Plus, you know that your little girl has been larger than life since the day she was born, and she only gets better with each passing day. You just need to prepare yourself for it."

Two big silver metal gates clashed together, causing a loud bang. This was the sound of Asia and her co-worker locking up the store for the night. After making sure the building was secure, Asia proceeded to walk towards the bus stop in front of the building, where she saw a small silver car driven by a younger man blasting loud music.

Hey, you want a ride?" her co-worker asked.

"No, I'm gonna wait on the bus. I need some time to think," Asia answered.

"OK, thinker. See you tomorrow," her co-worker said as she opened the front passenger door of the silver car. "Actually, I won't see you tomorrow. I'm off tomorrow."

"Well, lucky you," Asia remarked.

The coworker smiled. Happily, she said, "Yep! You'll be all alone. Don't miss me too much!"

"Girl, please." Asia gave her a side-eyed look.

"I know you will, acting all stank. BYE." her co-worker said as she got into the car.

"Bye."

Asia sat at the bus, waiting while reflecting upon her very busy day. For some odd reason, everybody wanted to shop today. While there were many things that crossed her path, she couldn't help but still think about where her life was headed and what exactly she wanted to do. She wondered how exactly someone like this lady who Nicole mentioned, Blac, could do to help her figure it out. A very shiny black Genesis G70 Coupe with four women inside pulled up at a red light; interestingly, these women looked very familiar to Asia. They happened to be the ladies who came into the clothing store earlier that day. Nicole was in the back seat; the slender, petite brown lady was in the passenger seat; and the driver was a slightly older woman with really curly, black, shoulder-length hair and very distinctive mahogany facial features. Her eyes were brown and slanted; she looked *too* familiar. *Do I know this woman?* Asia asked herself. *Only God Himself knows.* As she tried to get a better look at the driver, her phone rang. She quickly tried to silence it to focus on the driver, but when Asia looked back up at the car, the woman in the passenger seat was already looking at her.

"Hey! Thank you for the outfits!" the brown woman exclaimed.

Asia screamed back at the young lady, "You're welcome! Anytime!"

"Hey Blac," the young woman continued, "that's the girl who dressed us today. We got our stuff out of that store." She pointed to the store.

The driver looked up from her phone and at Asia with the coldest, deepest stare a person could ever give another. Maybe she looked at Asia that way because she saw Asia as a weird mirror image—a younger, less fortunate, innocent version of herself. The driver, after about ten long seconds of staring, attempted to speed off without taking her gaze off of Asia. She was soon cut off by a dirty pickup truck with cut down trees and branches in its bed. She slammed on the brakes to avoid running into the back of the truck that cut her off.

"Blac!" the passenger screamed.

Blac apologized and said that everything was fine, while Asia got onto the bus and wasn't even phased. One would think that she didn't even see what happened, which is a fair assumption. She didn't react, not because she didn't care, but simply because she was not focused on what was happening with the car and the woman. It was safe to say that Asia was deep in her thoughts. The bus driver pulled up behind Blac's car, and seeing this in her rearview mirror,

Blac turned to the young woman in the passenger seat.

"Do you know the young lady at the bus stop from anywhere else besides the store?" she asked.

"No," the brown woman said, "But I think Nicole do." Blac turned right after driving four blocks and the black sedan disappeared. The next morning, a sexy Blac sat at her small chrome and glass breakfast table in a white room adjacent to her kitchen. She greeted Nicole as she approached the table.

"Good morning, beautiful," said Blac.

"Good morning, Blac," Nicole replied. She sat down in front of an array of toast, eggs, bacon, orange juice, milk and butter and poured herself a glass of orange juice.

"Nicole, tell me something," Blac said, looking at Nicole inquisitively.

"Yes?"

"Who was that at the bus stop?" Blac asked.

"Oh, that was Asia," Nicole stated.

"How do you know her?"

"Well, we went to grammar school together. We were actually really good friends then, but our lives took two different directions and we never kept in contact. Why you ask?"

"Just curious," Blac explained. "She looked too familiar to me."

"Yeah, she looks like a younger version of you," Nicole laughed.

"No, really."

Nicole nodded her head as she bit a piece of toast. "She really does."

That means she's just pretty, anyway," Blac said. "I'm about to get ready to head out. I got a couple of meetings, so please make sure my domain is locked up before you leave."

"You know I always got you," Nicole assured her. Blac got up from the table in her morning lingerie and left the room. After breakfast, Nicole got dressed and went to PBE.

"Hey you," she said to Asia.

Asia looked up and stopped pricing clothes. "Uh-oh, what did we do wrong? What are you missing? Did you need something else?"

Nicole said, "No, I came to see you," with a sneaky smile on her face.

With a sense of relief, Asia sighed and turned back to the clothes. "What's up?"

"Oh, nothing," Nicole said. Just was wondering if you thought anything about what we discussed yesterday."

Asia smirked. "Yeah, I definitely thought about it, but Nicole, I don't know. I just don't know."

"Well, I can understand your hesitation," Nicole said. "I mean, I was the same way at first, too, but you'll get over that part. Plus, it might make you feel better to know that Blac asked us about you."

Asia stopped pricing the clothes once more and turned to look at Nicole. "She did?"

Nicole nodded. "Yeah, she did, this morning at breakfast. She asked me who you were and if I knew you outside the store." Asia's eyes widened. "That can't be good if she asked who I am."

Offended by Asia's sarcasm, Nicole rolled her eyes. "Well, if she asked who you are, that's definitely a good thing, because she don't just ask who random people are," she said with an attitude.

"But I think she only wanted to know who you were because you reminded her of what she looked like when she was broke and lost."

"Well, I guess she was a cute broke girl," Asia replied.

"I wouldn't know because I've never seen her broke, but I'm not gonna twist your arm about it. We are having a dinner party tomorrow. I just wanted to drop the address off and let you know that you are invited. You got a piece of paper?"

Asia reached into her supply cart and gave Nicole a piece of paper and a pen.

"I'm just gonna write the address down," Nicole said. If you see fit, just come by. You don't gotta dress all crazy fancy. It's a regular dinner party, but if you got, like, a dress and some sandals, that'll be cool. It ain't really that serious."

"I don't know, Nicole, "Asia said hesitantly.

"Girl, I'm not twisting your arm, and I'm definitely not asking for your kidney," Nicole explained. "I'm just gonna leave you with this paper, and if you decide to come, you know where to come. OK?"

"OK, Nicole."

Nicole put the paper and pen in Asia's cart, turned on her heels and exited the store. Asia picked up the paper. She twisted up her lip and rolled her eyes while looking at the address, then stuck the slip of the paper in the back pocket of her jeans.

Later that evening, Asia went home, where she was accompanied by her television and her black cat, Bell. Asia sat in the center of the couch with her legs crossed Indian-style and with a big bucket of popcorn. Sitting on the coffee table next to the couch was a tall mug of tea and on the couch armrest was Asia's work uniform. Bell jumped onto the couch and knocked the tea on Asia's uniform.

"Bell!" Asia scolded the cat as she jumped off the couch. Asia's phone started ringing. It was a FaceTime call from her best friend, Chloe.

Asia picked up the phone and propped it up on the counter while she loaded her PBE uniform into the washing machine.

"What you doing, hoochie?" Chloe asked excitedly.

"Nothing, whore!" said Asia.

Chloe laughed. "Ya mama!"

Asia laughed and said, "Her, too. But anyway, I ain't doing nothing. Washing clothes, thanks to Bell."

"Don't do Bell!" Chloe exclaimed. "What Bell do to you?"

"Well, *Bell* just spilled tea on my uniform, and now I gotta wash it."

"Why? You gotta work tomorrow?"

"Yup, but I ain't going," Asia said. She felt around the pants pockets. "Shit," she mumbled.

"What you looking for?" Chloe asked.

"I'm looking for this… paper…" Asia explained, trailing off as she searched.

Asia walked out of the room with her uniform pants in her hand and began to walk through the house, picking up and moving things.

"Asia!" Chloe called out.

"Girl, keep yo' virtual drawers on," Asia said as she walked into the kitchen. "Oh, here it is!"

"What? What were you looking for?" Chloe asked.

Asia picked up her cellphone and the piece of paper from her kitchen counter, then held the paper up to the camera. "This," she said.

"What's that?"

"It's this lady who got a bunch of money's address."   "You like old women now?" Chloe asked, laughing.

"No, hoe." Asia retorted.

"Well, it's obvious you don't want to tell me, so I don't care," Chloe responded bitterly.

Asia laughed. "Aw, don't get your panties in a bunch. I'm not telling you so you can judge me. Plus, I don't even know much about her; all I know is she got money and connections, and I want them."

"Well, be careful," Chloe warned her.

"Always," Asia said. "Oh, since I got you on the phone, you can help me pick something out."

"OK."

Asia sat her phone on a stand where Chloe had a perfect view, then went into her closet and pulled out three different dresses. "This one is Prada, and these some boujie people I'm meeting tomorrow," Asia explained.

Asia pulled out a teal, tight-fitting, knee-high Prada dress. The second dress she showed Chloe was a floral, backless, ankle-length dress. Both of these were very nice dresses, but they did nothing for her figure, which is probably why they were in the closet collecting dust. She pulled out one more dress and tried it on.

"Yassssss, bitch. That's the one!" Chloe exclaimed. Asia seemed to like the way it looked as well. "Yup, we got a winner," she confirmed. She took off the dress and put her comfy clothes back on.

"Well, how do you know the lady?" Chloe inquired.

"I don't know her," Asia explained. "I don't know if you remember Nicole, but we all went to school together."

"I don't know. I gotta see her."

"Yeah," Asia continued, "me and Nicole was really close, but we went to separate schools after graduating and never kept contact. But yeah, these her people. I don't know what PBE gon' do tomorrow, 'cause I won't be there."

"Did you call in?" Chloe asked.

"Yes, ma'am."

"OK, now."

"Let me get off this phone," Asia said. "They beat me up today. I'll call you tomorrow."

"OK, bye."

Asia cleaned off her bed, lit her candles, played her meditation music and laid down. She started to wonder what Blac would be like. Asia's mind raced with anticipation until she fell asleep.

Asia walked up the street looking at the paper, which told her she was getting close to the house. The sidewalk was made of fine brick that didn't resemble the rest of the street, and the grass was a pretty shade of green with really tall palm trees growing from it. Asia saw a brick wall that seemed tall enough to stop anyone from climbing over. She approached a pair of brass gates that had the initials "BB" engraved in them at the center where they connected. She looked down at the piece of paper to confirm she was at the right address and that there she wouldn't be chased away by two big men in black for trespassing. Her eyes weren't lying to her—the address on the house matched the one on the paper. Asia stood in the brick driveway amongst four thick, polished brass poles that sat in the middle of it; between two of the brass poles was a cement wall, and in the middle of this wall was a triangle-shaped rose gold electronic device with a speaker at the bottom. Asia walked up to the speaker, looked at it and looked around. She took another look at the piece of paper in her hand. She opened it once more to confirm she was at the right address. She looked back at the cement wall, walked closer to it and pressed a green light-up button with a phone symbol on it. After she pressed the green talk button, a voice instantly said, "Yes?"

"Hello, my name is Asia. I'm here to see Nicole."

"OK. Why are you here to see Nicole?" the voice within the device asked.

"Well, my name is Asia and Nicole invited me to the dinner party," Asia explained.

"You're a little early."

"Yes, yes, ma'am," Asia said, "but I didn't wanna get lost, so I just came in. Is that OK? If not, I can leave and come back."

"No, no, no, just come in," the voice said. Asia no longer heard the voice, but she now heard a dial tone. Two automated gates slid apart to open to reveal a palace; the brick driveway continued up to the front door and formed a circle around a big, beautiful running fountain. *This driveway seems to never end*, Asia thought, *but I'm sure this trek would feel quicker if I was in a car.* Speaking of cars, two really nice ones sat on each side of the fountain. She got to the front door, where she walked up three brick stairs to face two large cherry oak doors with glass windows that she could see straight through and a gold brass door handle that twisted to open.

Nicole greeted Asia at one of the doors.

"Hey, you showed up," Nicole said, excited and shocked. "Yeah, I'm here," Asia said. "Oh, my God, this place is like a music video house or a movie house!"

Nicole laughed. "Yeah, it's gorgeous here," she said, "and the rooms are amazing as well. It has a bunch of really cool places throughout it; it's real nice. Anyway, I'm glad you showed up."

"Well, I hope I'll be glad I showed up, too," Asia replied. She stood in the doorway wearing a peach cocktail dress that showed off her figure just enough, with some silver sandals to match.

Nicole laughed and said, "Girl, ain't nobody worried about you."

Asia looked up as she admired the high ceilings and the beautiful details. "How do I look?" she asked as she turned to Nicole. "You're fine," Nicole said. "You have on a dress and shoes, Asia. I mean, it's not gonna be a bunch of people here, and ain't nobody judging you off your clothes. Not to mention, people only gon' pay attention to you if you do stuff to bring attention to yourself. This dinner party is about to be full of people showing their gratitude and trying to get close to Blac while scarfing down her food and filling up on her liquor. Most people just gon' be here because they want something from her, but you'll be fine if you don't be doing anything to bring extra attention to yourself, which I'm pretty sure you won't 'cause you so scary for some reason."

"Shut up."

"Anyway, you'll figure it out."

Nicole and Asia walked into a room to the side of the hallway area near the front door. When they entered, there were two women standing inside. One of them was a light, bright woman with freckles on her face. She wore a nude-colored, classy, yet casual dress. On her neck was a pearl choker necklace and her hair was pulled back with a black headband atop of her head. A notebook was in her hand in which she seemed to be jotting down everything the other woman said. The other woman was the lady who almost tore up that pickup truck the other night; she stood talking to the freckled lady as she wore a long, peach-colored fitted sundress with her hair pinned up into a French roll with a swooped bang. She had on a pearl choker necklace as well, but hers happened to be filled with diamonds throughout, and she wore diamond earrings and bracelets to match. Asia's eyes caught the fancy diamond-encrusted watch on her right wrist. The ladies continued talking as Asia and Nicole entered the room. Asia was kind of nervous and Nicole looked at her slightly, putting her head down and subtly using her hands to tell Asia to just be quiet. They stood there until there was enough pause in the ladies' conversation to interrupt.

When that happened, Nicole spoke up. "Hey, Blac. This is Asia, the girl who works at PBE and my old grammar school classmate. She's gonna come to the dinner party, if that's fine."

Blac looked at the two young ladies standing in her dining area and chuckled. "Okay, boss lady, but that's not the way it works," she began. "You ask the host *before* the guests arrive, not when they're standing *in front* of the host. You ask *prior* to the event if they can come to the event; you don't invite the person, have them ring the bell and then ask if they can come. Not cool. That's like somebody going to the store and picking up groceries, taking them home, eating them and then coming back to pay for them." Blac paused, shook her head, sighed and said, "But anyway, she's cute. She can stay."

Blac looked at Asia and took several steps towards her until they were both staring each other in the face as if they were looking in the mirror.

"Hi, I'm Blac. Asia, is it?"

CHAPTER 3
STANDING STILL IN A STORM/
FRESH MEAT

Mirror, mirror, what do I see? A woman standing, looking just like me. Identical features come through; you are me and I am you. We are the same person, from our heads to our shoes.

Blac and Asia were mirror reflections of each other. Blac was stunned at the younger, innocent version of herself. While Asia was uncomfortable with this mature, well-poised woman who was making eye contact with her, this woman happened to have the same features as Asia. I mean, they had the same rich brown skin color, the same deep, slanted exotic eyes and, most of all, they both had figures to die for.

Asia looked at Blac, cleared her throat and said, "Yes, my name is Asia. You have an unbelievably beautiful home."

Blac smiled. "This is not my home," she said. "This is everybody's home, but thank you. I put a lot into it to make it the way I wanted it." She looked around. "I kind of think it paid off, wouldn't you agree?"

"Oh, yes, very much so," Asia said very quickly, agreeing with Blac.

Blac looked at Nicole. "I like her," she told Nicole. "She is kind of scary, which makes me nervous, but I like her."

"I'm sorry for just inviting her," Nicole said. "It will not happen again." Then, trying to lighten the mood, she said, "She's not scary. She's just nervous."

Blac looked at Nicole and said, "Oh, I know it won't, because you know better. And I don't know why she's scared of me. I'm just a person just like her; I just happen to be a person with a whole lot of money and power. I should be more scared of her than she should be of me."

Nicole rolled her eyes at Blac's sarcasm. "Well, it's a little early, Asia," she said, "so we can probably go and hang out in my room until it's time for the dinner party."

As Blac looked up, men in white shirts brought in beautiful bouquets of flowers. One of the men walked right in between Asia and Blac.

Blac looked at Asia. "Well, thank you for coming," she said. "I look forward to your company tonight at the dinner party."

"Thank you for allowing me to be here," Asia replied. "Is what I have on OK? I don't have many dress clothes."

"Yes, what you have on is perfect," Black answered as she looked Asia up and down, admiring her beautiful features from her head all the way to her toes.

"I'm a little busy getting ready for this dinner party, so I'ma let you girls go," Blac said. She turned toward Asia. "You are more than welcome to follow Nicole to her room and just hang out for a couple of hours before the dinner party starts."

Asia and Nicole nodded at Blac and left the room.

Nicole and Asia walked up a long flight of stairs—50 stairs, it seemed. When they got to the top of the stairs, they made a left, where they met a long hallway with multiple doors. Nicole opened one of the cherry oak doors, and inside was a big, beautiful room that contained everything a woman could possibly need. There was a king-sized bed that was topped with a fuzzy purple blanket, pillows—lots of pillows—and clothes. The room also had a flat screen TV mounted on the wall across from the bed, and off to the side was a tall dresser. Across the top of the dresser were photos of Dorothy Dandridge and Marilyn Monroe, surrounded by jewelry box and perfumes. Across the room next to a door was a beautiful makeup vanity atop which any makeup a woman could possibly dream of sat. Lip gloss, eyeliner, mascara, blush—*anything* a woman needed to get dolled up, it was there. It reminded Asia of backstage vanity at a fashion show. It was beautiful. This vanity caught Asia's attention because she really enjoyed makeup, so when she saw the vanity and all of the different makeup products, she fell in love. She mentioned nothing to Nicole, but instead just looked around the room and took in what she saw. Nicole looked up from her phone, then walked towards her bed and sat on it, pushing the clothes cluttering it to the side.

"Sit," Nicole said.

Asia sat on the bed in front of Nicole and asked, "Am I tripping, or did Blac steal my whole face?"

"I don't know who stole whose face," Nicole said, "but I already told her that y'all look too much alike."

"Fa' real! Wow, this is your room?" Asia gawked.

"Yeah, this my room… when I stay here," Nicole answered.

"What you mean, 'when you stay here'?" Asia asked.

"Yeah, girl, I don't live here," Nicole said. "I got my own house. This house is entirely too big, plus, I don't always be here. I come here every now and then, like if Blac's here or any other girls are here, but we all got our own houses. None of us stay here. This is like our play land. More often than not, if we're here, we have events and parties and things of that sort, but nobody really lives here."

"Oh, so this is just like the Playboy mansion or something?" Nicole laughed. "No, but it's pretty close," she said. "So, what do you think of Blac?"

"Well, she's beautiful, and I could have told you that from the other night," Asia answered.

"Yes, she *is* beautiful," Nicole agreed." I just can't wait for y'all to actually have a real conversation and for you to *really* get to talk to her, because you're going to fall in love with her. She's awesome. She's understanding and she knows a lot about life. Like, she don't talk about stuff she don't know, and she's not, like, shallow. She's very welcoming, you know? I mean, she cold to other people, but when it comes to us—the girls—she's really good. I've never seen her, like, treat a girl any type of way. I've seen girls get crazy with her, like trying to fight her and talk smack to her, and she don't even give them the time of day. She just has them removed, and when she sees them, she looks right through them like they don't exist, like she don't see them."

"Wow, they be trying to fight," Asia remarked.

"Yeah, her mouth crazy, but she don't argue with her girls," Nicole explained. "She say what she wants, and what she say, she means. Can't be no punk in this business. That's why most girls just stay out the way. She got all these people and all these horny, nasty men who know her. They know she always keeps a bunch of pretty females around. So, when they bring up certain females or talk about certain stuff they looking for, especially when they come from out of town, they hit her up. Then, she contacts the girl who fits the occasion or criteria, they pay her and she pays the girl. The girl does what she does and goes back to her life."

"That simple, hun?" Asia asked. "Girl, stop."

"Ain't nothing simple," said Nicole, "but this ain't complex, either. Now, if a girl wants some help with getting out the house or something like that, then, of course, she helps. She don't want us out here making her look bad because we're supposed to be getting all this money, yet our priorities ain't in order or we ain't got nothing to show for the work we do. So, she gets us together. But as far as her being a part of our everyday lives, that girl got too much going on. Plus, she be up under her man, so outside of business, she don't even be having the time to pay too much attention to us."

"Her man?" Asia asked. "She got a *man*?"

Nicole looked at Asia with a side-eye. "Yeah, she got a man. You think a woman *that* fine don't got a man?"

Asia sat back on Nicole's bed, crossed her legs and said, "I thought she was gay."

Nicole laughed. "Don't get it twisted," she said. "She loves the ladies, but she ain't gay; she's far from it. She probably likes and has had more men than you."

"Oh, I believe you," Asia said, laughing.

"I mean, don't get it twisted. She likes what she likes, but she *loves* her man," Nicole explained. Interested, Asia looked at Nicole.

"Will he be here tonight?" she asked.

Nicole shook her head. "No, he will not be here tonight." She lifted her head and looked at Asia. "Nobody besides high-ranking businessmen and street guys know what he looks like," she said. "A big-time gangsta' and a hoe," Asia said. "I guess they a match made in the slums."

"Wrong again!" Nicole said, defending them. "Blac ain't been a hoe in about 10 years. Listen to how you sound! A man *that* exclusive with a woman who's accessible to everybody, picture that."

"Well, I guess y'all make her a lot of money," Asia commented, "or she made a lot during her run."

"We do well," Nicole said. "From my understanding, she had a good run as well, but I wouldn't know. When I met Blac, she was already established and had a couple of girls."

"So, she must know what she's doing," Asia observed. "She definitely knows what she's doing," Nicole agreed, "and that's why that old man Charlie wears her out every chance he gets."

"He's old?"

"I don't know," Nicole replied. "I just assume that he is, but what I *do* know is that he changed her life, and she respects him for it."

"See," Nicole continued, "the beautiful black Bonnie, who we identify as Blac, had a big-time mobster as her Clyde. He goes by Charlie. He met her at a time when, instead of running the business, she *was* the business. He quickly changed that, which made her quickly find different ways to achieve her goals, become more hands-on with her vision and not be the product. No one actually knows what he looks like. Most people only know his voice; he has a really deep, distinctive voice. While how they met, who he is and even how he looks is a mystery, Blac adored him. For some reason, when she talks to him, whether he's cussing her out or showing her love, she can't stop smiling from ear to ear when they're talking. She always talks about him and how she gotta get home to him. Even though no one knows what he looks like, whoever he is, people don't play with him. He's very influential to Blac's success. If somebody messes with her and she don't wanna deal with it herself, she makes a phone call, and within minutes, that person is in big trouble. Don't nobody mess with Charlie."

Asia exhaled. "This seems like a movie."

"Girl, because it is."

The two girls continued to laugh and talk. Nicole continued to involuntarily spill Blac's business to Asia, who soaked it up like a sponge and became intrigued by what Nicole said about Blac, her lifestyle and the things she did.

Music played and people danced everywhere as Asia walked down the stairs to join everyone else who had already started parting and mingling at Blac's intimate dinner party. This was an elite dinner party; Asia saw lots of beautiful women dressed in gowns and the men looked dapper as well. There were all different types of servers—all races, all genders—walking around with trays of food and drinks. The servers wore all-black attire: black shoes, black pants and black button-down shirts. This was a *really* nice event. The room where Blac and Asia had met hours before the event was decorated with white lilies, white roses and silver crystal gems. From the ceiling hung a very big and beautiful crystal chandelier. As Asia entered, she saw the beautiful, curly-headed Blac. Blac's dress was an over-the-shoulder black diamond dress with a slit that rose all the way up to her panty line and a black diamond brooch that connected at her waist to keep the dress together. This dress was *beautiful* and it showed off her very voluptuous curvy figure. As Blac walked past Asia, she greeted one of the guys attending the party, sticking her neck out as he kissed her on her cheek. She smiled and thanked him for coming as she was pulled in multiple directions by other guests. She sat down at the head of the table, where beautiful girls sat to the right and left of her. She unfolded a napkin and put it on her lap as one of the servers came over and filled her flute with champagne. She smiled, laughed and talked to people as they walked up to her, greeting her and thanking her for such a nice event. So, Asia guessed that what Nicole said was true—it seemed like everybody was trying to get close to Blac for one reason or another.

Asia noticed herself continuing to stare at Blac and watching what she was doing at her section of the dinner table. Asia and Nicole weren't sitting very close to her, but they weren't far away, either. Asia tried to loosen up a bit and not stare so hard, but she couldn't help it after the stuff that she had learned about her earlier and with how damn *fine* she was looking. Blac kept catching Asia staring at her, and as she spoke to people, their eyes would meet. She would look at Asia, then look away very calmly to pay attention once more to what she was doing or talking about. Nicole very rudely interrupted Asia's thoughts.

"Hey, I need you to loosen up," she said.

Asia looked at her, squinting her eyes. "I *am* loose," she retorted.

Nicole looked at Asia, put her right hand over her chest and said, "Ma'am, you are *not* loose." They both laughed and Nicole continued, "No, for real, because I see Blac looking at you. I don't know if it's because you keep staring at her or because she's peeping you out to see what you do in this type of atmosphere. So, just loosen up and try to be normal, even though you're acting like you can't."

"OK, OK, OK, OK," Asia said. "I'll loosen up."

Nicole rolled her eyes and turned to her right, where there was another girl sitting next to her, and began talking to her.

Asia picked up her fork to take a bite of the food that was on her plate, but she wasn't really hungry. She didn't seem to have an appetite, so she instead picked up the glass of champagne that was in front of her and started to drink. *Hopefully, by drinking, I can get a little buzz, and that will make me loosen up a bit*, she thought. Almost immediately, she had finished the entire glass. Standing behind her was Blac. She stood over Asia, and Asia couldn't see her body. She sure *did* see, however, one of Blac's legs popped out of the dress, which revealed the fact that she wasn't wearing any underwear. *That's none of my business*, Asia thought.

Blac looked at Asia and said, "Well, you were *thirsty*." As she spoke, the girl sitting to the left of Asia stood up and pulled her chair out as Blac sat down next to Asia. "Are you enjoying yourself?" she asked.

Asia cleared her throat and said, "Yes—yes, ma'am. I'm—I'm OK."

"Relax," Blac said. "I don't bite… unless you want me to." Asia looked at her with a shocked expression.

She started laughing and said, "I'm joking, relax. I'm joking, I'm joking. Trust me, you're not my type. I prefer my fish richer in color and taste not to mention shorter than you." As Blac panned the room with her eyes, Asia looked away nervously and started playing with the food on her plate.

Blac looked at Asia once more. "Well, I'm glad I can afford to feed you, because you sure is playing with your food," she said. Asia put the fork down and apologized for playing with her food.

"No apology is necessary," Blac said. "Come take a walk with me."

Asia looked at her. "OK," she agreed. She wiped her mouth with the napkin that had been sitting in her lap and left it on the table.

Asia and Blac walked out of the room as people were speaking and continuing to greet her. Asia had no idea where they were going; she tried not to make it so obvious, but stayed close to Blac. It was almost as if Asia wasn't there because the other guests were only speaking to Blac, and they didn't even acknowledge her, but she was okay with that. They walked through the kitchen and approached a door that was, of course, cherry Oakwood. As they got closer to it, Blac entered a code and the door opened by itself. The room seemed like a secret room or something; Blac held her hand out and a voice said, "Welcome." Asia walked into the room and stopped in the doorway.

Asia observed the room; it looked like a wooden cabin. It was spotless, with shiny wood floors, black leather furniture and a library. Everything in the library was cherry oakwood, from the bookshelf all the way to the desk. The chair was made of black leather and next to it was a black metal coat hanger stand with a black hat atop it.

The bookshelf was filled with books and magazines, mostly fashion magazines, but she had a couple of literary magazines as well. Asia felt pretty sure that Blac didn't have time to read all of them, though. Next to the bookcase was a fireplace that was not lit. It looked like it had never been lit before, but it was cute, and it contributed a nice ambience to the room. Across from the fireplace was a couch with a long coffee table in front of it.

There was nothing on or under the coffee table. This room was very well-kept; Asia could tell. She could also tell that not everyone wasn't allowed to be in here, which somewhat gave her the vibes that she shouldn't be in there, either—this mentally brought Asia back to her mother's "sunroom." While her mother was not the most spiritual person, she believed in spirituality and she followed a lot of teachings; she also had a sacred area in her home that she called her sunroom. This was the room where she would go to read literature about spirituality, light candles and speak to her ancestors, her beloved mother and her father. In her sunroom, she had a really big picture of her parents together. This photo was surrounded by candles, incense and a pair of pearls. This room also had a bookshelf, but it was nowhere near as expensive as Blac's. Asia's mother's bookshelf had the Bible, mason jars, candles, seasonings and bottles of Florida water on it. These were all tools that she would use as she learned along her spiritual journey. She was in various groups that were filled with people who once were seekers of understanding and soul healing as well.

These groups helped to give Asia's mom faith and guide her soul here on earth. Later in life, Asia learned what she used the items for. Earlier on, however, she never thought to ask her mom, and she was only allowed to go into the sunroom when she and her mom would recite Psalms 91 and "Our Father," the prayers of protection. Asia's mom would let her come into the sunroom every night to get on her knees and say these prayers before bed. So. Asia understood what it was like to be welcomed into a sacred place and how it was inappropriate to enter unless invited or unless there was a specific reason. *What was Blac's reason for inviting me into her sacred place that looked like a library?* Asia wondered. She didn't know, but she was sure about to find out. Blac interrupted Asia's rampant thoughts. "Excuse me, ma'am. Can I come in?"

Asia moved out of the way so that Blac could walk in. Blac walked into the room and shut the door   "Sorry, it's kinda loud out there," she said.

Asia looked at Blac and said, "You have a beautiful room."

"Thank you," Blac said, looking at Asia. "I love it; it's probably my favorite place in the whole house sometimes. It reminds me that it's OK to just exhale and get away from all the chaos of the world."

"Oh, I know," Asia said. "My mother had a very sacred room in her home. When I was growing up, she would pray, light candles and mixed herbs. Then, you know, she'd do things that were healing to her soul."

"So, I take it you understand and know that being able to take care of yourself on a more spiritual level is important, "Blac said. "It's refreshing. It's good to know that you're spiritually inclined, or you at least have some spiritual teaching," she added.

"Oh, definitely. My mother didn't play, and she taught the importance of emotions and feelings."

"Yeah?" Blac asked. "And what about your father?"

"Oh, my father *really* didn't play," Asia explained. "He was more of, like, a disciplinary to him structure with standards, and rules were everything."

"Good. Well, that tells me you can follow some direction," Blac commented.

"Huh?"

"You heard me?" Black asked, then continued: "That means you can follow some direction. So, your mother was spiritual, which means that she would probably was or is nurturing. And your father was disciplinary; he was the head of the household and he taught structure, which means that you, my dear, know how to follow directions." She walked in front of the bookshelf, turned around, looked at Asia and said, "When you truly follow your gut and your instincts, it screams out at you when you're put in certain positions—or, should I say, situations. So, what was your gut saying when you got up to follow me into this room?"

Asia said, "I'm not sure what my gut is telling me. What *should* my gut be telling me?"

"Well, you're seeking me for a reason," Blac replied. "For what reason, I don't know, but I heard that you were seeking me. I just figured that I wouldn't waste my time or yours, so I would get to the bottom of it sooner rather than later."

Asia said, "I think that's funny, because I was actually introduced to the idea of you by Nicole."

"So, you didn't ask?"

"Well, yeah," Asia explained. "After she told me different stuff about you and what you did, I wanted to know more, but originally, I didn't know nothing about you."

Blac sat behind the cherry oak desk. "Girl, please. You been hawking me all night. You been staring at me harder than some of these men. I almost charged you a fee the way your eyes were glued to my cat when I was standing over you. But I ain't tripping. You was definitely one of many tonight." She folded her hands together.

"OK, so, what do you wanna know?"

"I *don't*. I mean, I'm not sure what I wanna know," Asia replied.

"Do you know what I do?" Blac asked.

"Yes, I'm fully aware of you and what you do, madam."

"No, you're not," Blac stated curtly.

"Cause if you did, you would *never* call me 'madam.' I *hate* that term."

Asia quickly fixed her words and apologized. "I'm sorry. I didn't mean to offend you."

"I have tough skin," Blac said. "It takes a lot more than a word to offend me, but I wanna know about you. I don't know why, but I kinda like you, so I wanna know about you."

"Well, it's not much to tell about me," Asia began. "I'm 21 and I just finished my LPN program at—"

Blac stopped her. "A nurse working at a clothing store? Did I miss something?"

Asia looked at Blac and said, "Well, I didn't really like the companies I was working for. I just worked for them for the experience, so I quit being a nurse. Plus, I didn't really like the way I was going about it all, so I figured I would give it a break and try something different. If it's meant to be, I'll go back to it."

"That makes sense," Blac said. "Every now and then, we have to refocus, but I'm pretty sure you could have got a job doing something else other than working at the clothing store. I'm pretty sure you don't make a lot of money there."

Asia looked at Blac. "I make enough," she said defensively. "You don't make enough, 'cause if you made enough, you would be at work instead of in my house drinking and playing with my expensive food."

"I'm kind of intrigued by your lifestyle," Asia said. "It seems very entertaining."

"Everything that glitters ain't gold. We work real hard."

"I'm pretty sure of it."

"So, you're a nurse working in a clothing store, and what, you have other goals? You wanna do something different, so what exactly do you wanna do?" Blac asked Asia.

"Now, that's the issue," Asia explained. "I'm having a hard time figuring out exactly what I want to do next in life."

"Well, you better figure it out fast, because time waits for no man. Before you know it, life will have passed you by. You won't have anything accomplished—that's why setting goals and executing them is very important." Blac said.

Asia nodded and agreed. "Well, I don't wanna go work back at the clothing store, and Nicole kinda told me what you do, and I'm kinda interested in that type of work," she said.

Blac looked at Asia. "Are you sure?" she asked, then took a serious tone. "Because this is the grown people game, and I don't have time to invest time and money into someone who's gonna wake up tomorrow, say she's done with it and just walk away from me. I don't have that type of time or patience." she explained.

"No, I really am interested!" Asia exclaimed eagerly. "I'm pretty sure that if I learn everything, you'll be happy that you taught me."

"Oh, you pretty confident," Blac said, surprised.

"Well, I'm cute," Asia said, "and if I learn what to do, then I should be OK. Plus, if you use houses like this just to have events and parties, this is *definitely* something I want to get into. I mean, I like big houses and jewelry, too."

Blac scratched her head. "It's so much more than meets the eye, especially if you think these people 'bout to just be waiting in line for you because you got a pretty face. Sometimes, that money is harder to get than it should be. But if you say you ready for something like this, then who am I to doubt you? Anyway, it's getting late. I'm not gonna have you go all the way back home tonight; plus, we got some interesting characters at the party, and I don't want nothing to happen to you while you leave. So, we got a extra spare bedroom upstairs that's not too far from Nicole's room. You could stay in that room tonight. There's a bathroom, and everything you need is accessible in there, so you won't have to leave if you decide to take a shower or bath or anything of that sort. I'll have Nicole get you ready with some pajamas and anything you may need to turn in for the night. Just see Nicole, and then in the morning, I'll have the girls gets you together for the masquerade party," she said.

"Masquerade party?" Asia asked.

"You hard of hearing, or is you a parrot? Are you repeating everything I say?" Blac asked her in return. "Don't do that! *Like I said*, I'll make sure you right for the party. Then, there, I'll decide if you ready for this, depending on how you receive the people at the masquerade party and the way you handle the things that you may see. Don't embarrass me with any of the horror movie looks you have been putting on tonight. If you can't handle adult fun and games, you might as well not even come."

"I'm a big girl. I can handle myself," Asia responded.

Blac said, "So, we'll see tomorrow. After it's over, we can

talk about you possibly going on a trial run to see if you can live up to this lifestyle."

As Asia thanked Blac, a really hard knock at the door interrupted them.

Blac looked at the door and said, "Somebody has lost their mind."

She flung the door open, and there stood a very big man who looked like a barbarian caveman. He was *huge*. He looked like something out of a horror movie. She opened the door.

"What is wrong with you, knocking at this door like that?" she asked him.

"My bad, Blac," the man standing in the doorway said," but we got a problem."

"Nah, homie. *You* got a problem. *You* better handle it. Don't involve me," Blac replied.

"Casey drunk," the man explained. "She getting in girls' faces and they arguing, and you know I don't get into the girl stuff." Blac shook her head. "I'm sick of y'all. I'll be out in a sec," she said.

While the man was talking to Blac, Asia noticed a small silver gun sitting on the bookshelf. Asia was not sure why Blac felt like she needed a gun, but the idea of drama happening at the dinner party scared her. *If this is happening at a dinner party, I definitely want to be ready for anything that might happen at the masquerade party*, she thought. Blac stopped the man.

"Stop. Stop talking," Blac told him. "First of all, where is your home training? I am in here with somebody."

"Oh, I didn't even see her," the man said. He turned to Asia and said, "My bad, Miss. He looked at Blac. "She cute."

Blac turned to Asia. "This, unfortunately, is my head of security. His name is Bo. You ever have any issues with anybody? That's who you wanna see," she explained.

Bo co-signed Blac's introduction. "Hey, yeah," he said. "I'm the one to call, unless it's another female you got problems with. So, if you talk smack, I hope you can throw hands. 'Cause if you can't, you gon' get beat up and I'ma watch. But I'ma take you to the hospital afterwards, though."

"Bo, what is that to tell somebody?" Blac asked Bo, sucking her teeth.

"What? I'm just keeping it straight," Bo replied. "What you want me to do, Blac? Lie? OK. If you have any problems, come get me. Because the girls *will* try to fight you, even though you cute with some double Ds touching yo' chin."

Blac said, "You just a pervert," pushed Bo out of the doorway and slammed it. She looked at Asia and continued, "Ignore him. He has been dropped on his head too many times."

Asia laughed at Bo. She then told Blac that she appreciated her letting her stay and that she was looking forward to the masquerade party.

Now, Asia had never been to a masquerade party, but she had read books and watched movies about masquerade parties. All she knew was that at masquerade parties, a lot of people walked around and everybody seemed to have on these masks that covered their eyes. She also knew that these were people who had money. So, she was pretty sure that everybody there would be wearing really nice gowns and really sexy tuxedos.

Blac and Asia left the library and rejoined everybody else at the dinner party. They all laughed and danced all night long until they either fell asleep or got their drivers to take them home. Asia ended up getting a little tipsy, but not *too* tipsy. She was a little buzzed from the champagne, so she decided that she had consumed enough and was ready to turn in for the night. She looked around the party and saw that huddled up in a group of three females and two males was just who she was looking for. She got Nicole's attention. "Hey, I'm tired," Asia said to Nicole. "Can you show me where the room that Blac said I could sleep in?"

Nicole nodded her head and agreed to take Asia to the room. After entering the room, she pulled out a T-shirt and sweatpants and gave them to Asia.

"So this is what you wear," Nicole instructed her. "Towels, washcloths and soap are in the bathroom if you wanna take a shower.

And if you need anything, just text my phone."

"OK," Asia said. Soon enough, she passed out in the bed.

Asia awoke from her slumber and stretched as she saw a nosy Nicole staring out of the window of the room in which she was sleeping.

"Well, good morning, Sleeping Beauty," Nicole said.

Asia squinted her eyes, blocking the sun. "What are you doing here and what time is it?" she asked.

"Ma'am, it is 1 p.m., and I'm in here to make sure you ain't dead."

"I ain't dead."

"Yeah, I see that. Blac wanted me to come up here and make sure you weren't dead because you slept for a really long time. I would not have heard the end of it if I would have brought you here and you died."

Asia looked at Nicole. "That's a little harsh," she commented. I gotta die?"

"The way that dinner party ended, you never know," Nicole replied. "But you're very much alive. You probably don't have a bed as comfortable as this one at home, so your body just was a victim." They both laughed.

"Yeah," Asia agreed. "This *is* a really comfortable bed... or was I just drunk off that champagne and couldn't get up? Wait, how did I get this T-shirt and sweatpants on?"

"Beats me," Nicole said. "I gave them to you and then I left. I seen you was already passed out before I left the room, so I locked you in. You can only unlock the door from the inside, so you must have gotten up in the middle of the night and put those clothes on. I don't know. I was drunk."

"You must know I thought somebody came in and undressed me."

"I don't know what you were thinking. I'm just telling you what I saw."

"Because you apparently know I put on the clothes by myself."

"Yeah, I know you did, 'but I know what you were thinking cause you crazy," Nicole said. "But anyway, you can leave that on unless you uncomfortable going outside with clothes you slept in. We gotta go shopping and get ready for the party tonight. I'm in charge of your look, and you will *not* embarrass me."

Asia looked at Nicole. "I'm not putting that dress back on, so I definitely will be wearing this T-shirt and sweatpants. And you *wish* I could ever embarrass you. Oh, and why you ain't tell me about the masquerade party?" she replied.

"No, ma'am," Nicole said, shaking her head. "You ain't getting me cussed out again, especially with the way you people watch. No way, Jose."

"OK. I get it. Plus, Blac invited me, anyway, and you still stuck with me," Asia teased, sticking her tongue out at Nicole.

"Whatever," Nicole said, rolling her eyes. "Let's get it together." The two ladies left the mansion and headed to the shops to find themselves some really cute costumes.

CHAPTER 4
DARK GAMES/IMPULSIVE ACTIONS

Yells and laughter filled the air throughout the mansion; women were giggling and running around. Everyone there seemed to be dressed up in extremely sexy clothes with masquerade masks on their faces, just as Asia projected based on what she had seen on TV. A young, 21-year-old Asia stood at the top of the stairs with a black, long-sleeved lace gown that flowed all the way down to her feet. She wore black four-inch heels that had diamonds 'round the toe and ankle straps, as well as a very cute, but classy, silver diamond necklace with matching earrings. Her hair was pulled up into a bun with her baby hairs laid. Under her dress, she wore a red lace bra and red lace boy short-style panties that completely covered her privates. She also wore red lipstick. She looked mesmerizing. At the bottom of the stairs stood a woman who revealed all of herself in a sexy black mesh dress that hugged her body in all the right ways. The dress included diamonds which covered her nipples and bikini area. She had a *curvy* figure, so nice that it would only be fair for her to reveal most of it. She was the center of attention—what better way to become the focus of the party other than to basically have on a black mink coat with literally nothing under it besides the mesh material and sparkling coverage? The woman was almost completely naked, but her outfit—the mesh and diamond dress with the fur coat—would definitely stand out on a clothing rack.

Still standing at the top of the stairs, Asia made eye contact with Blac. Blac, while holding what looked like a glass of champagne, smirked and nodded at Asia, beckoning her to come down the stairs. Blac was surrounded by three men who appeared to be talking to her, but they stopped and stared at Asia as she began walking down the stairs. Asia descended the stairs very slowly because she had never worn heels before tonight, but she was *not* going to let herself fall in front of these people—especially not Blac. As Asia reached the bottom of the stairs, one of the gentlemen spoke to her.

"Hello, beautiful. I don't remember seeing you before," he said.

Asia started to reply, "Um—"

"For a good reason," Blac interrupted the interaction. The man put his hands up in defeat and backed away from Asia.

"Asia, are you comfortable?" Blac asked.

Asia replied, "Yes, I'm very comfortable."

"Well, don't be a stranger," Blac instructed her. "Mingle, go around the room, see what's going on and enjoy yourself. That's what tonight's basically about, enjoying yourself, 'cause trust me, everybody here is going to enjoy themselves."

The man sucked his teeth as he looked at Blac's attire. "I know I'm gonna enjoy myself," he commented, smirking.

Blac looked at him. "Only in your dreams," she replied.

Asia entered the living room, which looked like an adult Candy Land. It almost looked like an adult playground; there were so many half-naked women and shirtless men running around. Asia grabbled a corner to see exactly what was going on, as the lights were out. The living room was pitch-black, and all she could hear was people screaming and running. The lights were turned back on and Asia could hear soft giggles. Everyone seemed to be hiding. A voice called out.

"Misty!"

A woman wearing a yellow silk gown and a yellow mask stood up. "Hmm?" she replied to the voice.

A tall, sexy, bald chocolate man scooped her up. "Gotcha," he said.

Misty covered her face as the fine man scooped her up and carried her to the couch. She covered her face in embarrassment as he lifted her dress, opened her legs and buried his face between her thighs. The woman uncovered her face, reaching for anything

54

she could grip while rolling her eyes to the back of her head. Her mouth was open, with sexy sounds coming out. As she looked down at the man, she stopped reaching and instead put both her hands on top of his bald head. She bit her lip and tilted her head back as her body shook. Asia then realized that the party guests were playing a game. This appeared to be a game in which the women were being captured by the men. They would turn the lights off and the women would run around the room. When the lights were turned back on, whichever woman was unable to hide in time would be captured by a man. The man would lift it up her skirt, if she was wearing one, and his head would disappear beneath it. Asia was shocked by what she was seeing, but she knew that she could not visibly react to what she was seeing because she was pretty sure that Blac was somewhere watching her facial expressions or having someone else do so. Asia played it cool and acted like she wasn't fazed by what she was seeing, but she made sure that she stayed far away from the players so they wouldn't mistake her for a part of the fun.

Asia moved throughout the party, seeing what people were doing and what atmosphere she was getting herself into. There were people kissing, there were people dancing and there were people running around. There were men running around and grabbing the ladies, so as she walked toward the stairs, she grabbed a glass of champagne because she knew that she *definitely* needed to loosen up if she wanted to enjoy this party. *This party is worse than the one they had last night*, she thought. Asia walked upstairs, where more people were hanging out, and on her way there, she saw people hanging out on the stairwell.

Upstairs seemed to be even more exciting. The upper level of Blac's home had seven rooms, most of which were set up to accommodate the fetishes of the elite. The room where Asia had slept the previous night happened to be the only room that was not being used. Each room had something different taking place inside, and Asia stood at the top of the stairs to see snippets of what was going on in the rooms. The doors to the rooms were like revolving doors; none stayed open long enough for Asia to fully see who was in which room doing what. One of the doors opened and a woman came out with a man to go into another room. In the room they had just left, there was another man strapped to what looked like a dartboard with restraints around his neck and hands. Asia was shocked, so she drank her champagne a little bit faster. *This seems to be a freak fest,* she thought, *but everyone seems to be comfortable.* Based on Asia's observations, everybody seemed to be OK with everything and was enjoying themselves. Asia sat in the hall near the stairs, where she watched everything that was going on. In one of the rooms, though, one of the girls was in trouble. And this time, Asia could see everything that was happening.

This young woman was one of the escorts who were working the rooms upstairs. She stood at five feet and three inches and weighed 90 pounds oak and we. Her hair was pulled up into a high ponytail with Chinese-style bangs that almost completely covered her eyes.

"Sam, stop grabbing me by the back of my neck," she said. She was being aggressively handled by the man in the room.

"Girl, come here," the man, who Asia assumed to be Sam, said. "Where you going?" he asked her. He was an older man and he was blatantly intoxicated.

"Sam, stop," she demanded. "You being too aggressive. I don't like that. You might need to get you somebody that's into that."

"No," the man refused. "I want your sexy little chocolate self."

The woman pulled away from the drunk old man and pulled out her phone. Sam forcefully pushed her back against the wall. "Listen to me," he said. "I done paid Blac my money, so you ain't going nowhere. Matter of fact, gimme this phone."

"Sam, gimme my phone," the girl pleaded, reaching for her phone. Sam grinned.

"I like them feisty," he said. Then, he ripped her shirt and started grabbing her breasts.

The young woman started to yell. "Stop, Sam!" She kicked him in his nuts and dashed out of the room with half of her clothes torn from her body.

Asia wasn't sure if this woman wanted her clothes ripped off or not, but it surely didn't seem like it. She was very frantic and ran to one of the other rooms, but the door was locked and she couldn't get in. She banged on the door for two seconds before dashing past Asia, looking straight in her face and then quickly looking away. She began to go down the stairs, but unfortunately for her, Blac was still standing in the same spot she was in when Asia first came downstairs. Blac looked at her and gave a glare that could only be described as the look of death. Nicole was right—Blac don't play. The girl abruptly turned around, went back up the stairs and went into one of the empty rooms. This just wasn't sitting right with Asia; she could just tell that everything was not OK with this woman. The woman ran into another room, then back to the empty room, so Asia ran into the room she had slept in the night before, grabbed the gun from the bookshelf, and went into the room that the girl was in. She busted through the door and the woman jumped.

"I'm sorry I scared you," Asia began, "but are you OK?" "*No*, I'm not OK. I'm so sick of these drunk fools," the woman replied.

"What happened?" Asia asked.

"I was in the room with the man because he was my date," she explained, sniffling. "All of a sudden, he started choking me and ripping off my clothes. I told him that I didn't like what he was doing and he told me he wasn't gonna play with me. Blac ain't giving no refunds. I told him that I was not into that type of stuff and that I would find him another girl who was, but no. Drunk Sam didn't want to hear that. He continued ripping my clothes off and trying to put his nasty mouth on me, so I kicked him in his nuts and ran out of the room. I went to the other room because that's the room Bo's stationed in. He got cameras; he supposed to be watching everything that goes on, but clearly, he ain't watching because he would have seen that happen."

"Somebody needs to tell him to do his job," Asia agreed. "What was he doing?" she asked.

The girl looked at Asia. "Your guess is better than mine," she said.

What these two young ladies didn't know was that Bo was in the room with the security cameras, but he couldn't seem to keep his eyes open long enough to pay attention to them. His mandingo was touching the back of Saesy's throat, so he surely wouldn't see what the cameras were capturing.

When the woman knocked on the door a few moments prior, Saesy had lifted her head and asked Bo, "You heard that?"

Bo looked at the door, dazed. "Heard what?" he asked before sucking his teeth and answering before thinking. "Nah," he said as he pushed her head back down.

Saesy resumed moving her head up and down, sucking Bo's mandingo as if she was trying to pull smoke from a hookah. He looked down at her, grunting and saying, "Yeah."

Asia looked at the distressed woman. "Well, did he pay you?" she asked.

"They don't pay us. They pay Blac," the woman explained, returning Asia's gaze.

"Well, you should be OK, because, from my understanding, she makes them pay," Asia reassured her.

"Yeah, but he took my phone," the woman replied, concerned.

"He took your phone?" Asia asked.

"Yeah," the woman said. "He took my phone when we were getting into it. He said he was gonna give it back when we were done because he's high-profile. He wanted to make sure I wasn't gonna record him, so he took it, but I don't care who he is or what he does."

"Well, do you wanna go get it?"

The woman, full of emotions, looked at Asia with a defeated expression. "*Go get it?*" she tersely asked, dumbfounded by Asia's naïve question. "Did not just hear me tell you that he was ripping off my clothes, practically acting like he was about to rape me? Now, *you* wanna go in there?"

"I am not afraid of him," Asia responded.

"Well, I do want my phone back," the woman said, contemplating a game plan…"So, yeah, we can go in there together. It might be better if both of us go."

So, the pair approached the room where Sam remained. The upset woman entered first. Sam looked at her and laughed.

"Blac must'a sent you back," he said smugly.

"I'm not 'bout to deal with you," the woman replied with newfound strength in her voice. "I just came to get my phone." "You ain't getting nothing from me. You just kicked me in my nuts and I'm gonna have to go to the hospital," Sam responded, waving her away with his words.

"Well, if you had stopped when I asked you to, I never would have kicked you."

"Well, I ain't giving you no phone back. I know Blac ain't giving me my money back, so the least I can do is keep this phone as a souvenir."

Asia walked into the room at this moment. "You not keeping her phone," she said, defending the woman. "Give that girl her phone back."

Sam was taken aback as he looked at Asia. "Oh, you sexy," he commented aloud, licking his lips. "Who you is, a shero here to save the day?" he asked mockingly.

"Don't worry about who I am," Asia told him. "Who I am ain't important. But what you got to do—what you *gon'* do—is give this girl her phone back."

"I ain't giving her nothing," Sam refused. "Ain't nobody gon' make me give her this phone back."

"You wanna try your luck tonight?" Asia asked.

"Girl, you don't look like you can hurt a fly," Sam said. "I ain't worried about you, and y'all together can't take me." As he finished talking, he lunged forward to attack the other girl. Asia shot him in the back of the head. The girl moved out of the way as the man fell onto the carpet. Asia stood there, frozen, completely shocked by what had just happened. She was shocked that she had even shot him; she had never shot anybody before. She had never even been in a fight, so she didn't understand where the strength to do that came from, and she *sure* didn't know what was about to happen next.

The other girl screamed. "We gotta find Blac," she said in a panic.

The girl ran out of the room screaming Blac's name. "BLAC! BLAC! BLAC!"

Blac looked up from the bottom of the stairs to see who was screaming her name. When she realized it was an emergency, Blac came upstairs and came into the room. She saw the man laying facedown in a puddle of his own blood. Asia was still standing with the gun in her hand, standing over the man, just looking at him. Blac closed the door.

"What happened?" Blac asked. Asia looked at her.

"He was gonna hurt her, so I shot him," Asia explained.

"OK, you shot him. Give me the gun," Blac demanded.

"Blac, I didn't mean to kill him," Asia continued. "I—I don't even know why I shot him… I just thought he was *really* gonna hurt her."

Blac looked at Asia and shook her head. "I get it," she said. "I understand. I'd rather *him* be dead than *her*. Just give me the gun." Asia gave Blac the gun and slid down the wall as she looked at Sam's drunken, now dead body. Blac pulled out her cell phone and called someone.

"Hello. What are you doing?" she said into the phone.

"I'm doing nothing," the voice on the other line responded.

"I need you in this room right now," Blac stated.

"What room?"

"Three doors from the stairs."

Blac hung up the phone, and within two seconds, the person she was on the phone with had busted into the room. It was Bo.

"Oh, my God!" Bo exclaimed. "What happened?"

The victim of the attack turned to Bo. "This crazy fool was trying to rip off my clothes and he practically raped me! I went to go get you and I couldn't find you," she explained. She then turned and pointed at Asia before continuing. "This girl seen me running up and down the stairs and going into other rooms, and she asked me what was wrong. I told her what happened and we came back in here to get my phone from him. He said he wasn't gon' give it to me and he tried to ambush me and... you know... he got shot."

Blac looked back at the poor girl, rolled her eyes and looked back over at Asia. Asia looked absolutely devastated. Blac walked up to Asia and grabbed her hand.

"Don't worry. I'll take care of it," she said.

This was the beginning of Blac taking care of Asia and fixing her problems. Blac couldn't possibly forget Asia after this encounter. Blac walked Asia into the room where she had slept the previous night and began to run her bathwater. Blac helped Asia undress and put her in the bathtub. Asia looked at Blac, her face filled with sorrow.

"Don't look like that," Blac said, looking right back at her. "Don't worry about it. I'll take care of it. I just need you to relax your mind and get some rest. If you feel okay to, you can come back downstairs, but I think that after this encounter, this might be the end of your night."

Asia sat in the tub, soaking and asking for forgiveness for what she had done. So many thoughts ran through her head: *What's going to happen next? Am I going to jail? Will someone else try to kill me because of this?* She was so uncertain about anything that could come after this situation because she had never experienced anything like this before, but Asia remembered something that she had learned from her mom. Silvia had taught her that when a person's mind is racing and full of thoughts, the best thing for them to do is attempt to release all of their mental clutter as best they can. So, Asia did just that. She released her thoughts and tried to relax her mind. Shortly after, she got out of the tub and went to bed. She wasn't completely relaxed, but of course, she wouldn't be—how does one completely relax after shooting a man in the back of his head and committing cold-blooded murder? Of course, it would be a little difficult for anyone to relax immediately after that. Eventually,

Asia fell asleep at around 6 a.m. Hours later, she awoke to go to the bathroom, but instead of using the one in her room, she decided to travel through multiple areas of the house. She wanted to be nosy and look just to see what was going on, but the house looked nothing like she expected it to.

The house was like a ghost town. There was no one on the couches; there was no one in the living room. There were no people there, and everything was clean. The home, in no way, looked like a crazy party with naked men and women running around had taken place in it hours earlier. She went through the kitchen and saw a dim light coming from a room off to the side. Asia walked through the door to this room, where she immediately thought, *This must be Blac's room. It has to be.* This room was huge. When Asia walked into the beautiful room, she noticed pictures of Blac and other Hollywood movie stars from the 1940s and 1950s, like Eartha Kitt and Lena Horne, throughout the room. The furniture in the room was tasteful; it was soft pink with white and gold accents. Asia noticed Blac's king-size canopy bed, which had a soft, white, diamond accented headboard and a bed frame with gold trim lining it. There were golden post on each corner of the bed, which upheld a sheer, glittery, pink and gold curtain-like cloth. The bed had lots of pillows all over it; the bed was neatly displayed and made up. It looked like a display room inside of a home magazine. Nothing seems to be out of tact.

Asia continued to walk through the room very quietly and headed towards the bathroom, where there was soft music playing. The light that she had seen from the kitchen got brighter as she approached the bathroom. That wasn't the only thing Asia noticed as she got closer to the bathroom—there was a grinding noise, comparable to that of a drill. This noise was so loud that it overshadowed her thoughts of the night before. Asia very slowly and silently crept to the door, stood in the doorway and peered into the bathroom. Asia stood at the door as she saw that numerous candles—she thought the total number seemed to be over 100— were lit and arranged throughout the bathroom. The grinding noise had now become extremely loud. There was a woman kneeling on her feet and leaning into the bathtub, which was filled with a red liquid. The woman had a drill in her hand, and beside her lay three big knives that were covered in the liquid. The drilling stopped and the woman turned around to look at Asia. Asia's eyes widened in shock—Blac was staring back at her, without a flinch, without an inkling of hesitation or regret. Blac was on her hands and knees, leaning over the bathtub, drilling through and cutting up the body of the man who Asia had shot and killed just moments earlier. Blac, while looking at Asia, held the drill up in the air and pressed the button, causing it to whir once again. She then turned her attention back to the tub and started drilling through Sam again.

Asia ran out of the room and up the stairs. She was in shock. Up until now, she hadn't known exactly what she was getting herself into. She had previously learned that Blac was in charge of an escort service, which seemed fine and cool. She was now learning, however, that Blac was *very* hands-on with disposing of and getting rid of issues. This scared Asia, but it also intrigued her. Asia felt safe with Blac—likely because she knew that if anything happened to her, Blac would be by her side and able to protect her. At this point, Asia knew what Nicole had been talking about. Asia now knew that Blac would take care of anything. What a trial run that was.

The next afternoon, Asia was sitting at the table in the sunroom of Blac's house. This is where the ladies would gather or, in Asia's case, eat lunch and snacks alone. This was the same table where Nicole and Blac had eaten breakfast and spoken about Asia days before. Now, she was in the same seat, reflecting on her thoughts and the chain of events that had taken place the previous night. A sexy Blac came down the hall as if she was walking down the runway. She wore a yellow bodysuit with pink heels, her hair was curled as usual and she had black glasses on her face. Asia failed to hear or see the diva coming, as she was deep in thought. Blac walked into the sunroom and stood behind the chair Asia was sitting in.

"BOO!" Blac shouted. Asia turned around, startled.

"Hey, Blac," Asia replied.

"You scared, hon?" Blac asked.

"A little," Asia said.

"Well, you did kill Sam in cold blood?" Blac inquired.

Asia's eyes got big. She lowered her head down to the table in shame. "Shhh. I didn't mean to shoot that man and you know that," she said.

"No. YOU 'shhh.' Don't hush me in my own house. *You* did it. Listen to what I'm saying, or you can go out into the world and deal with what you did, and I *know* you don't want to do that. Plus, ain't nobody here but me and you," Blac said. After a short pause, she continued.

"Well, you did what was necessary, which is cool. He was going to hurt her, so you hurt him. No problem, but the problem is this: Y'all should have let Sam have that phone and let me deal with him myself. Instead, you wanted to be the 'iPhone Hero.' Now, you got a body, and I got Sam's blood on my hands. You clearly need some guidance, because if you knew anything, you would know to choose your battles. That wasn't a war worth fighting. I could have bought that girl a new phone, but I can't bring Sam back. You had me up all night cutting up body parts something I haven't done in years. I don't even like period blood, let alone a dead man's blood. That ain't even the kicker. The kicker was that instead of enjoying the entertainment from somebody's cute chocolate daughter who was on my heels all night, I was in my beautiful powder room playing with the limbs of a dead trick. Did it freak you out when you came into my powder room?" Blac looked Asia in the eyes, annoyed and angry.

"Ye—"

"Good!" Blac cut her off, irritated. "Don't just be peeking around corners and going into rooms you haven't been invited into. You lucky I was in the bathroom with Sam and not swirling my tongue around the happy place and butt of somebody's daughter, but *I* wasn't so lucky. Oh, and don't cross me. I ain't nothing to play with. I am the pretty gangster not to be toyed or played with."

"Who, or what, turned you into a killer?" Asia asked naively.

"Don't matter," Blac answered tersely. "Learn how to control your emotions. And, most of all, don't touch a thang in this house without permission, because I know that's my gun you used." Asia lifted her finger. Blac put her hand up to stop her foolishness.

"Don't you dare lie, or I'ma put you out," she continued. "Stealing? Ma'am, that is *stealing*. Next time, I'ma cut your fingers off, and you done seen me in action, so you know I'll do it."

Asia put her hand down and just sat there, looking out the window. The two ladies sat in silence for a moment before Blac placed her hand over Asia's.

Sometimes in life, you just gotta roll the dice," Blac explained. "While rolling that dice, you don't even know what you're doing. So, you live, and you continue to make mistakes while trying to get wherever you're going, but you don't stop. You keep going until the timer stops. See, you haven't lived, so you don't even really know what mistakes are. With the route you're on, you'll learn real fast— you see what you did to Sam. You already learning."

Blac squeezed Asia's hand, then let go, sat back in her chair and exhaled.

CHAPTER 5
SPARKLING THANGS/EXOTIC KISSES

Blac walked into the room where Asia was daydreaming. "Hey, what you doing?" Blac asked her.

Asia quickly turned around and said nothing.

"What you was in here doing, daydreaming? I told you not to worry about it. I got you covered. But anyways, come take a ride wit' me. I gotta get you out the house,"

Blac instructed her. "Where we going?" Asia asked.

"Out!" Blac explained. "Out to enjoy one of my favorite pastimes. And from the look of things, you could use some therapy, too."

Asia and Blac headed downstairs and out the front door. Parked at the entrance was a black metallic, wet-looking Rolls Royce with chrome on the trim of the car and rims of the wheels. A man wearing all black opened the door for Asia, who stood in front of the car. Her eyes followed Blac, who walked to the other side to meet another man, the driver. Blac looked at Asia as she stood there like an ice sculpture.

"Get in!" Blac yelled. "What you waiting for?" She sucked her teeth and got in the car. The two men closed the doors, entered the car then drove out of the residence and into the world.

Blac looked at Asia. "Look, I got something specific that I need you to do for me," she said.

"What's that?" Asia asked.

"I need a secret weapon," Blac said. "I need something that's easy on the eyes, but your worst nightmare that you don't see coming."

"I don't know about that," Asia said hesitantly. "Sam shook me up pretty bad."

"You ain't shook up too bad," Blac retorted. "You going to shop."

"That's where we going?" Asia asked.

"Yes," Blac replied tersely. "What, you thought I was taking you to meet Beyonce?"

"I wasn't expecting to go shopping," Asia said, putting her head down meekly.

"Me either, but based on your wardrobe, you could use this trip," Blac responded.

"It's nothing wrong with my clothes," Asia replied in a huff. Asia was becoming sick of the sarcastic, belittling tone Blac took with her. She was taught to take responsibility for her actions, which is why she let Blac have her way, but she wasn't about to sit there and keep catching the shade Blac was throwing.

Blac looked at Asia. "Look, it may seem like I'm beating upon you," she said, "but that's not the case. I need you just as much as you need me, so I'ma do my part, and I just need you to do the same."

"But I don't know much," said Asia.

"That's cool," Blac replied. "That's why I'll teach you, if you'll let me. But all jokes aside, I need you to come in this mall with me so I can show you how to dress the part." "OK... I guess," Asia hesitantly agreed.

"You trust me, don't you?" Blac asked.

"Sure," Asia responded.

"I'll take that."

The two women went into the mall and visited multiple stores. Blac practically bought Asia an entirely new wardrobe. Blac believed that Asia had what it took to finish what she had started. While she had multiple girls who were loyal and worthy of this new power and acknowledgment, Asia was different. Asia had a sexy innocence about her, which Blac wanted to use to her advantage. In her circle, Blac had guys who looked like killers and gals who looked like hoes. Asia resembled neither, but had the potential to be both—under the right direction, of course.

After a long day of shopping, Asia and Blac sat down at one of Blac's favorite restaurants, Tamela's Brazilian Steakhouse and Seafood.

Asia said to Blac, "While I appreciate everything you're doing, I need a little time to take everything in."

"Girl, relax," Blac said. "I ain't trying to get you in my bed. Just eat."

"I'm not saying that," Asia replied.

Blac stopped her. "We have been conversing since we met," she said. "I'm tired. All I want to do is enjoy my nice little meal at one of my favorite places, if that's OK with you."

"OK… sorry…" Asia said meekly.

"No apology necessary. Just eat. We'll talk after dinner."

So, they did just that. They enjoyed each other's genuine company and made plenty of small talk while pushing the heavy stuff to the backs of their minds. After dinner, the driver picked them up, and Blac escorted Asia back to her apartment. As they approached Asia's apartment building, Blac grabbed Asia's hand and looked at her. Asia returned the look, unsure what was coming next.

"Look," Blac started, "the streets need order, and I need somebody to create it with me. Now, I can choose anybody for this task, but I want somebody who is undetected and who ain't afraid to get the job done—and that's you. So, basically, you learn and you conquer. It's a whole lot of things you can do, but seduction is yo' weapon and I'ma teach you how to use it."

"Well, can I have a couple of days to think about it?" Asia asked.

"That's fair," Blac agreed. "Hit me up when you figure it out. Oh, and think about what kinda car you want, because I don't like sharing mines when you should have your own."

"Yes, ma'am."

The man sitting in the passenger seat helped Asia to put her bags in her apartment, and when he returned to the car, Blac's driver drove off.

While Asia was putting her new wardrobe away, she received a FaceTime call on her phone.

"What's up?" Asia answered.

"OK, phew!" Chloe exclaimed. "I ain't talk to you in a couple of days. I thought I was gon' have to come looking for you!"

Asia laughed and said, "You wouldn't even know where to look."

"Whatever," Chloe responded. "What you doing?"

"Nothing. Just putting these clothes up," Asia said.

"OK, so, how was the party?" Chloe eagerly asked.

"It was cool," Asia replied. "The dinner party was really nice. Then, the next day, they had a masquerade party that was cool—at least, 'til this drunk fool started tripping."

"That's what you get for being grown," Chloe said, laughing.

"Girl, gimme a break," Asia responded. "If I had asked you to come, you would have been front and center."

"I like having a job and taking care of myself," Chloe retorted.

"What that mean?" Asia asked.

"You risk yo' job to go be around people who can't even hold their liquor," Chloe commented.

"Well damn, Chloe. Just judge everybody at the party, then."

"I ain't judging," Chloe explained, "but if that's what they was doing, you shoulda went to work."

"I wouldn't trade the party for a shift at work. For the most part, I had fun and I'm happy I went, so you just stick wit' yo' job and let me do what I do."

"OK, do it," Chloe surrendered. "Just don't say I didn't warn you."

"Chloe... I'ma call you tomorrow."

Asia didn't even wait for Chloe to respond before hanging up. She realized that Chloe definitely had to stay in the dark about the series of events that had occurred over the last couple of days. Chloe had her own reservations about this new interest of Asia's, and rightfully so. Asia and Chloe shared everything with each

70

other and had big plans to become successful together. Due to her curiosity about Blac's world, Asia's focus began to shift, and Chloe saw that early on. Asia could have sat and explained everything to Chloe. It wasn't like she didn't trust her; she just trusted *herself* a little bit more. This was because Asia was afraid of the judgment she might receive from Chloe if she knew some of the activities that had occurred, based on how she responded to the small bit of information Asia provided about the party. In other news, Asia had bigger fish to fry. She had to figure out what she was going to do next and how she felt about working with Blac. Besides, all of this could possibly affect her in the long run. The strangest thing about the previous night was that Blac demonstrated absolutely no remorse for the callous disposal of Sam's body. This was a bad person who was surely going to do something worse than what Asia had seen. These types of thoughts and justification gave Asia the comfort she needed to sleep well, and sleep well is just what she did.

About three days later, after pondering her predicament and weighing the pros and cons of her new lifestyle, she picked up her phone to make a call.

The line trilled, and soon, there was a voice on the other end of it—Blac's voice.

"Hello?" Blac answered.

"Hey, Blac. It's Asia," Asia greeted her.

"Hey, gal! What's up?"

"I think I'ma go ahead and get with you."

"OK, cool, Blac said. "And don't worry about that little problem—I got you."

"OK, thanks," Asia replied.

"I got you. Don't worry about nothing. Anyways, I need you to meet somebody, so I'ma send you a driver tomorrow at 2:00 p.m. Please be ready," Blac instructed her.

"No problem. I will be," Asia agreed.

"OK, later," Blac said in an attempt to end the conversation.

"Later?" Asia asked, confused.

"Yes, child. Later. I never say bye because bye is indefinite,"

Blac explained.

"OK. Later."

The two ladies hung up and went about their days.

The next day, a man in an all-black suit knocked at Asia's front door. *Knock, knock.* Asia opened the door.

"Hi, Asia. I'm your driver. Shall we get out of here?" the man standing before her asked.

"Sure," Asia replied. "I just gotta lock up."

The man stepped back. "Take your time," he said. Asia locked the doors to her apartment.

"Ready," she announced.

The gentleman escorted Asia outside, then stopped beside an SUV. He reached into his pocket, took out his phone and called someone who Asia thought, based on the conversation, was Blac. Asia's suspicions were confirmed when he turned to her and handed her the phone.

"Asia, here you go. It's Blac," he said. Asia took the phone.

"Hey, Blac."

"Hey, Pooh," Blac greeted her. "Listen, this is my last time sending you a driver."

"I understand," Asia said. "I'll figure it out."

"Ma'am, hush," Blac replied, chuckling. "What I'm saying is, that car behind the SUV with the pink bow on it is yours."

Asia looked past the SUV and saw a cute, black, two-door Tesla parked with a pink bow atop it. She looked at the driver, who held up a single key.

"Well," he began, "I'll follow you to the house so you can get familiar with it."

Asia went from shocked to excited. She looked at the phone, beaming.

"Blac..." she started.

"What, girl? I didn't know what you like, so I let Bo pick it out. He's lucky you like it, because if not, he was 'bout to be driving his big body in that little car," Blac replied.

"No, Bo has great taste," Asia reassured her. "I love it—like,

LOVE love it. Thank you so much, Blac!"

"Thank *you* for trusting my vision," Blac said. "Now, come. We are all here waiting."

Asia returned the phone to the driver. He walked her to her new sign-on bonus to joining Blac's family, then returned to the SUV. He signaled Asia to pull off, and once she did, he followed her in the SUV.

Asia and the driver, who had played her escort so well that he deserved an Oscar, pulled into the property and exited their vehicles. Asia thanked the man and the pair walked to the front door together. A young woman opened the door. She was dressed very conservatively and her hair was pulled back into a ponytail. She wore a white button-down shirt that had vertical buttons along the front, a skirt that went down to her ankles, and black closed-toed flats.

"Hey, big man," she said.

"Hey, Angelica," the driver replied.

Angelica looked at Asia. "Hi, Asia. I'm Angelica."

Asia looked at her, confused. "You know me?"

"It's my job to know everybody. I'm Blac's assistant," Angelica replied.

"Oh, hi," Asia began. "As you know, I'm—"

Bo entered the room, stealing Asia's spotlight. "Aaasssiiiaaa," he said in a singsong voice.

Asia laughed. "Hey, Bo," she greeted him.

"So, I see you've just met the most annoying and cutest creature on the planet," Bo commented.

Angelica looked at Bo. "Very funny," she said, crossing her arms and glaring at him.

Bo laughed. "I'm just playing," he assured Angelica. "Anyways, come with me, Asia. Blac in here?"

Bo walked Asia to the library, which she was already familiar with. What she didn't know, however, was that the library contained a secret room. When Bo pushed the bookshelf, it swung back to reveal an all-black room with a large table inside. The room was full of men and women, who all wore black clothing and extremely nice jewelry pieces. Some wore glasses. At the head of the table was no other than the queen herself—Blac.

Blac wore an all-black leather bodysuit with bedazzled six-inch heels made of hot pink leather. She accessorized with a silver chain, the pendant of which read *BLAC* in black and hot pink diamonds, as well as two diamond choker necklaces, a diamond ring and diamond bracelets. Blac's tightly curled, jet black hair sat on her shoulders and her makeup was flawless as per usual; she wore black lipstick that was further defined by black lip liner.

Blac looked at Asia. "Well, hello, beautiful," she said.

Asia returned Blac's gaze. "Hey, Blac. How you doing?" "I could be better," Blac replied. She looked away from Asia and projected her voice to get everyone's attention. "OK, let's get this started. First things first: I wanna thank everybody for everything that they've been doing. The numbers are looking good, the girls are looking good, the businesses are looking good. Everything's on the rise, so I just want to thank y'all for everything y'all do. I never want anybody to be able to say that they wasn't appreciated or that I never gave them their roses, so thank you. Next, I want everybody to give the newest member of the family some love," she said, turning to Asia before continuing.

"This is Asia. Asia is easy on the eyes, but she ain't nothing to play with. She loyal, smart and, most of all, she a killer. So, welcome, Asia. Y'all help her out and make sure she good."
Everyone in the room nodded their heads up and down, then greeted Asia and showed her love as if she had received an award. Asia truly felt like she was a member of the family. She actually felt pretty good because these were pretty important people—at least, in her mind, they were. So, if they acknowledged her and made her feel welcome, this was obviously a place where she was supposed to be. The noise and applause in the room ended and one of the men sitting at the table leaned in.

"Blac, we got a problem," he said.

Blac looked at the gentleman, twisting her face and rolling

her eyes. "What type of problem?" she asked.

The man took off his glasses. "Well, 'Big Man' Dave sent a message through a trick to one of the girls and said that he got some girls coming in town for the weekend," he explained. "He said he the only one who gon' be hittin' any big licks for the big weekend, so if you don't shut your operation down and take yo' girls on a vacay, he gon' shut it down for you."

"With what army?" Blac asked. "I'm not worried about Dave. Dave know he don't want to see me on his best day. He better sit down."

"You gon' have to sit him down, because he been going around telling people he trying to run you out of town. He been saying you had a nice little run and it's time for somebody else to have fun," the man said.

Blac laughed. "Somebody dimming my light ain't never been a problem of mines. I ain't never been worried about that," she replied.

Another man at the table spoke up. "Hey, so, it sounds like we gon' have to go see little buddy."

Bo looked at him. "Yeah? Good luck getting next to him," he replied sarcastically.

"Getting next to *me* is the issue," Blac said. "Dave is breakfast food, but one thing's for sure: I don't do stuff based on rumors, opinions or thoughts. He has to show me something in order for me to react."

Bo looked at Blac. "Yeah, until something happens that we can't take back," he replied.

Blac looked back at Bo. "What do you want me to do, leave his brains in the street? You know I don't even work like that," she responded.

Everybody in the room began talking over one another. The atmosphere became chaotic and Asia quickly realized that these people were not to be messed with. While no one seemed to be fearful, *everyone* seemed to be *aggressive*, and that was a problem. "Quiet!" Blac shouted. The room calmed down and she continued,

"Listen. I understand that everybody wants to protect what's theirs or stand in their position, but to go at somebody and start a full-fledged war because they jealous of us is ignorant and stupid. The best thing to do is be a big fish in a tank full of sharks." "Yeah," Bo said with a snarky tone. "Get eaten up if you don't watch what you doing."

Blac smacked her hand on the table in front of Bo. "Don't challenge me, Bo!" she yelled. "Don't let your emotions and arrogance put you in a trick bag." She panned the room and continued, "While Bo is speaking from the heart, he's neglecting his fucking brain. We gotta be as little of a threat as possible, then attack when they least expect it. You don't take the bait and show up without planning and preparing. You study, you get ready, you lay the groundwork. Don't be stupid! They know what they said. They know what threats they made. They know what they gon' put out there in the air. They expect some type of retaliation and they expect it to come full force at the front door. As much as I like to walk through doors and turn keys, sometimes it's OK to go through a window. So, let's get our emotions intact, continue to get money and live how we've always lived. Let me worry about 'Big Dave.' He's not ready, and as far as his girls go, *I* got all the big licks in the city. How you gon' have an elite clientele with bottom of the barrel hoes? Shit! That weekend would be a disgrace; nobody would *ever* come back to the city after that shit. I did too much—and I *do* too much—to let some jealous, nickel-and-dime pimp destroy the elite image I created for my people. I'm not having it, so y'all better get your emotions intact, and don't worry 'bout Dave. Let me handle that."

The room was now much calmer than it had been before Blac spoke. This woman had some high-level control—this was some cult-type stuff. Asia had never seen someone control a room and handle jabs the way Blac just did. Blac held so much strength and feminine power as she demanded respect, and Asia was in awe. Blac looked away, then back at everyone in the room. "Plus, we got bigger fish to fry," she said. "I'm not worried about nobody on the outside when we got problems on the inside."

Everybody looked at Blac with shocked expressions on their faces. There was no telling what she was about to say. *Is she about to mention Sam?* Asia thought to herself. She became nervous as everyone remained focused on Blac, eager to see what she was referring to.

"Yeah, pick up ya jaws," she said, rolling her eyes. "I got a problem! So, little Miss Claire got knocked."

Bo shook his head. "No!" he exclaimed, putting his hands on top of his head in shock. "How?! How did that happen?"

"No, no no," Blac said. "It was stupid. She clearly was out of pocket. She wasn't following no good direction. She took the trick to a different spot, she didn't make him empty his pockets when he walked into the room and she called me from her phone in the room."

In Asia's mind, Blac was a professor, and she was about to get schooled. The table disappeared and Blac became a sexy professor standing in front of a lecture hall and wearing a black, knee-high, tight-fitting dress with red six-inch heels. In her hand was a metal pointer. On her face was a pair of Versace reading glasses, and her lips were dressed in red lipstick. Blac's hair was styled in her signature shoulder-length 1950's curls. In Asia's mind, all of the other attendees in the room had disappeared, and she was the only student.

"The first rule of thumb is," Blac began, "never take tricks who are high in the elite to a Motel 6 or a cheap room. And if they say they wanna go to a cheap room, you cancel the date, because our clientele don't even like Motel 6 or cheap hotels. So, if this person wants a cheap room, you 'bout to get robbed or it's a setup of some type. Second, when you come into the room, you supposed to make them empty they pockets of all electronic devices. These are the people who don't want to be recorded, so if they don't want you to record them, why would you let them record you? While it's plenty of do's and don'ts, please *don't ever call me*. I'm the *last* person you should contact. But in this case, I was the *first* one to be contacted." Blac looked Asia deep in the eyes and pushed her glasses up the bridge of her nose. Then, Asia snapped out of her schoolroom fantasy, and the room went back to normal. Blac continued.

"So, Claire is on house arrest 'til further notice."

Bo looked at Blac. "I can't believe this happened," he said. "Not to go into too many details, but they basically tried to frame her and say that she was hitting a lick, when the reality is that they was transferring conversations between phones to try to have a case stacked against her. But I got people on it," Blac explained.

"Damn," Bo commented.

"No, it was stupid," Blac said. "If she would have took the client's phone and put it in the basket, as we always do and as I taught her to do, when he got in, she could have avoided that. More importantly, how were they able to prove who she was or what she was doing? Something ain't right about the trick or the police in that situation, so I'm looking into that as well."

One of the ladies at the table, who wore her hair pulled up into a top bun with diamond chopsticks sticking out of it and a Chinese-cut bang sat up. "Speaking of the police, Blac, you might wanna be careful," she said. "Word on the street is that the forces are eyeballing you and you're being watched by the Feds. They got some detective who's working on a bunch of the homicides in the city and she trying to figure out a way to prove that they attached to you."

Blac looked at Smalls, the woman who had just spoken. "Who is it?" she asked.

"I don't know the girl, but her name is Lola, Lo, something like that," Smalls explained. "I don't know her name, but she have, like, a thing out for you, and she claimed she gon' bring down the family, so just be careful with how you move."

"I'm not worried about that; that's why people get paid," Blac replied. "But I *do* need to figure out who this chick is and what her issue is. So, duly noted. Thanks, Smalls. But if nobody else got anything for me, let's wrap this up and get back to work. I can chat with you later. Bo and Asia, come up with me."

Blac pulled Bo to a corner as everybody else conversed and exited the library's secret room.

"Bo, let me explain something to you," Blac spoke sternly. "It's never a good idea to swing yo' nuts in one of my meetings. Don't let it happen again."

Bo attempted to explain his position, but she shut him down. "Saesy done sucked out the last few brain cells you got?" she continued. "Drop the ball again and you won't have to worry." Blac walked away, leaving Bo with something to think about. Blac and Asia walked out of the room and ascended the stairs, talking. As they reached the top of the stairs, Blac looked at Asia. "Listen, this ain't no little girl game and this ain't no fun," Blac instructed Asia. "Yeah, we enjoy our lives, and yes, we have a lot of materialistic things that people want, but we work hard for everything we've got. It's certain things you just don't do. First of all, when it comes to the outside world, you *never* call me. People ain't even supposed to know that we know each other. *Never* call me. If anything, I'll find you—*never* come looking for me. Second, don't *ever* do anything off of impulse. Don't hit no licks off of impulse just 'cause it look or sound good. Don't go see nobody off of impulse. You need to always make sure that you're the big fish in the tank with the sharks, because one thing for certain, two things for sure: Sharks are arrogant because of their larger size, and they fail to realize that fish can maneuver 'cause they're lightweight. Last, but certainly not least, make sure you *always* the baddest one in the room, because some reputations stand alone, and you ain't *never* got to speak a word. You hear me?"

Asia looked at Blac. "I got it," she said.

"I hope so," Blac replied.

CHAPTER 6
LEARNING LESSONS AND WEARING HEELS

Asia sat in her car at the park near her apartment. She wanted to figure out a way to impress Blac or let her know that she was worthy of being deemed important, but she knew that in order to get that type of respect and honor, she had to do something that was out of the box. Asia had to do something that was *impressive*. For some reason, she could not get Big Dave out of her mind. Asia wanted to know more about the situation, because while it wasn't a big deal to Blac, it was a big deal to the other people who had been at the meeting in the secret room. This made her feel like if she went ahead and took care of the issue with Big Dave, her initiative and determination would be demonstrated to Blac. Due to this, Asia thought, Blac would have gratitude towards her and think of her as more than just an impulsive hothead.

As Asia sat in her car, her phone began to ring.

"Hello?" she answered. The voice on the other end of the line was Nicole's. She was calling to be nosy because she didn't get to talk to Asia much after the meeting, as Blac had quickly grabbed Asia and left.

"Hey, girl! What you doing?" Nicole greeted Asia.

Asia said, "Nothing much, just chilling."

Nicole said, "I see you got a new car. It's beautiful."

Asia said, "Thank you. I was actually shocked."

Nicole said, "Why was you shocked? I told you, Blac will take care of you."

Asia paused for a second and said, "What are you doing?" Nicole said, "I'm not doing nothing; I'm just chilling out. Was thinking about going shopping. As a matter of fact, I'm hungry, so I'm 'bout to figure out what to eat."

"The timing couldn't be better!" Asia said excitedly. "Meet me at the seafood spot and we'll grab something to eat."

Nicole said, "I'll be there in 20."

Asia said, "I'm headed there now as well."

The two women hung up and began their conquests to meet each other. Asia invited Nicole out to eat because she knew that Nicole always ran her mouth about business that she shouldn't even be speaking of to begin with. Everything that Asia knew about Blac from outside of their one-on-one conversations had been learned from Nicole. So, if Asia needed any information, she knew that she could get it from Nicole. Asia set at the table and waited for Nicole to arrive. As she played on her phone and sipped water with lemon, Nicole approached the table.

"Hey, girl," Nicole greeted Asia.

Asia looked up, smiled and said, "Hey."

Nicole sat down and said, "Hey. Did you order yet?" Asia shook her head. "I was waiting for you, so I didn't order anything."

The waiter came by the table and both ladies ordered their meals. Nicole ordered a glass of water with a margarita—a lime one, to be exact. After about 30 minutes of chatting and small talk, Asia seized the opportunity to talk about Big Dave.

Asia asked, "Nicole, would you ever lie to me?"

Nicole said, "You put your pants on one leg at a time like I do. I would never. I don't have a reason to."

Asia said, "So, tell me about Big Dave."

Nicole said, "There ain't much details. He's a big financial investor that has a lot of money, so he thinks that he can do and say whatever he wants. But he better leave Blac alone, 'cause he gon' meet his match."

Asia said, "So, he's a financial advisor. What kind of financials?"

Nicole said, "Basically, companies that wanna start businesses, or people who wanna try to put a large amount of money in their businesses. He basically tells them if it's a good idea or not, and they pay him good money for his knowledge and expertise. But on the flip side, he's a guy who brings girls into town who basically go on dates with the elites. That's why he and Blac are in the same circle: He wants her to slow up her girls so that he can have some new girls from out of town come in and make some money. He don't wanna share. He wants these new girls to take over Blac's streets, and she's not having it, so we'll see what happens."

Asia looked at Nicole and said, "Yes, we will. So, what about this big weekend that everybody's talking about?"

Nicole said, "It's just a big financial business convention that a whole lot of people are coming into town to attend. It's supposed to be big money for girls like us." Both crumbs and words spilled out of her mouth as she educated this newbie.

Asia said, "Well, where is his building, then? If he runs a big company, it should be somewhere downtown."

Nicole said, "It's downtown. It's right downtown."

Asia just sat back in her seat, continuing to laugh and talk with Nicole as she soaked up everything Nicole said. Asia knew that in order to get any information about this man or get close to him, she would have to book a meeting with him. Asia didn't have any type of education as it related to financials or accounting, but she was a nurse, so she had a little bit of book smarts. So, she did what she knew to do first: She Googled him to find out information about him. When she typed in the address to the district office, "Davado" came up easily. She assumed that was Big Dave's whole name and remembered that sometimes, when a person is looking for stuff, other things just fall in their lap. While looking to book a meeting with Big Dave, a job posting for a temporary assistant position came across Asia's phone screen.

Now, this was something that Asia could do. She had experience in administrative work because she had to take a course on it when she went to school for nursing. So, all she would have to do is doctor her resume so that they would meet with her and she could gain the information she needed to know about Big Dave and ultimately get closer to him. The next day, while sitting at a coffee shop in the downtown district, she was drinking a mug of tea and eating a bagel while surfing the internet on her laptop. Asia quickly closed the window she was using and started a new search. This Google search brought Asia to the job offers at Big Dave's financial company, which provided her with an email address. She then sent over an cover letter and resume to this email address to express her interest in the temporary assistant position. Asia sent the email and continued to enjoy the ambiance of the coffee shop until she was bored enough to pack up and head home.

Asia got home and decided to prepare herself. She binge-watched court shows, as well as crime and murder shows, on the A&E channel, to learn different tactful ways to dispose of a dead body. While Asia wasn't a mass murderer, she was intrigued by the idea of being the one that another person wouldn't see coming, especially Big Dave. Asia was experiencing different types of moods and energies. This was all fairly new to her, but as she did before, she had to protect her people, especially Blac. While there was no doubt in Asia's mind that Blac could take care of herself, the idea of impressing Blac and getting her gratitude was exciting to Asia. While she might have reacted emotionally in the past, this was a completely new and different situation, and Asia was becoming more intrigued by what she could become. She was extremely enticed by the thrill of what was happening. It made her feel like she worked in the Secret Service or a similar agency. This gave Asia a sense of purpose and she loved it. There was a small coffee shop attached to the lobby of Big Dave's business building; Asia had learned this after researching Dave and his business.

While Asia was on her quest for information, Blac still continued business as usual—that is, until drama almost knocked her over as she walked through the intersection of a busy street. The gentleman who had almost tripped Blac was one of the high-profile lawyers in the city. While he had a real name, everyone called him Chin. He earned that nickname due to his very masculine face and deep, strong features, with a chin that hung down long, touching his chest. He was not the best looking guy, but he was definitely a gentleman and he dressed really nice. He bumped into Blac as he marched across the street with his briefcase in one hand and his cell phone to his ear. They then made eye contact as they both realized that they knew each other. Their initial reactions changed and they warmly greeted each other.

Chin said, "Blac! Hey, girl. Now, you know you gotta move out the way when you see a monster truck coming." He laughed and instantly put his phone away as he turned around to walk in her direction. They made it across the busy street and stood on the corner.

Blac said, "Chin, you just lucky you ain't hurt me. You know you don't want no parts of Prince nor Charlie."

Chin fixed his black Versace blazer and said, "Not even on my best day! Now, why would I think of doing anything to two of my biggest clients? I wouldn't hurt their most prized possession." Blac laughed and said, "Cut the shit. Stop gassing me."

Chin said, "Well, I *am* the biggest attorney in the city. Plus, you are definitely a diamond in the rough that Charlie managed to dig up. Lucky man."

Blac said, "I'll say."

Chin said, "Me, too. Hey, so you ready for Friday night? I know you got a fine stable ready."

Blac said, "I don't follow."

Chin said, "OK, play like you don't know if you want to. Anyways, I've been meaning to catch up with you, but I guess the Universe brought us together because I was taking too long."

Blac said, "What's up?"

Chin said, "You know Dave, right?"

Blac said, "Yeah, I know the dude." She rolled her eyes and twisted up her face.

Chin said, "Well, he sick of y'all getting all the big lick, so he talking about how you need to shut down by Friday."

Blac put her hands on her hips and said, "I'm really gonna have to put that dog to sleep."

Chin said, "I didn't hear that."

Blac said, "Yes, you did. And hear this, too, since the streets always relaying messages. You hear me loud like an intercom. I ain't shutting down *shit*!"

The gentleman looked at Blac and said, "Hold your horses, cowboy—or, should I say, cowgirl. I just thought I should give a friend a friendly heads up, that's all."

Blac looked at Chin and said, "I bet. You just answer the phone when it goes down."

Chin said, "Just make it a case I beat."

Blac said, "I always do."

Chin said, "Bet."

Both Chin and Blac stood in silence at the busy street corner. Blac was fuming.

Chin looked at Blac and said, "Well, I'ma let you go. It seems like you got a lot on your mind."

Blac snapped out of her thought and said, "Who, me? I'm good, but I'ma let you go, Chin."

Chin said, "It was a pleasure walking into you."

Blac said, "Like always, love."

Chin said, "You know I want you, right?"

Blac rolled her eyes and said, "So does Charlie."

Chin said, "Yeah, Charlie does, too. That's why he keeps you locked up."

They both laughed and went their separate ways. As much as she wanted to brush off Chin's weak advances at her, she couldn't shake the fact that someone who hadn't done or experienced the things she had wanted to cut the cord on her girls. This bothered Blac more so because she wasn't ready for a war. She tried her best to get her money and stay out of others' way, but sometimes, the fact that she minded her own business made her a target. She never asked for trouble, but she wasn't a stranger to handling it when it came, either. Blac already had a plan for Asia, but in her eyes, Asia wasn't mature enough or ready—at least, that's what she thought. Back at the coffee shop was Asia, dressed in attire similar to that of a secretary's. She drank green tea and surfed the web while watching the traffic around the building. While ear hustling to the conversations of the security guard who was directing and greeting people, she overheard him keep repeating, "Floor number 11." Asia wrote the number down in a notebook and proceeded to pack up her belongings. It was beginning to get late, and the traffic slowed, so she headed to her apartment.

Asia did this routine for about three days. During the process of very discreetly and patiently gathering information about the atmosphere of Dave's company building, she also read books and continued to watch documentaries about murder and the mistakes people commonly make. On the evening of her third night sitting at the coffee stop, she was at home binge-watching crime shows when she received an email alert on her phone.

This email was from the recruiting department of Dave's financial investments company. This was the access that she needed to at least get around some people who knew Dave. She was very excited as she read the email that contained details regarding an interview: "tomorrow morning at 11 a.m." As she read through the itinerary for the interview, she realized that the 11th floor was the floor where Dave's company was located. Then, she realized that most of the traffic in the lobby was from people who were going to visit the 11th floor. Asia sat back in her bed as she took in the fact that she was really about to gain some type of access to Dave's company. While she wasn't sure how much access she would receive to Dave, she was just excited to have accomplished this completely on her own, with her own life experiences and with the vague lessons that being in Blac's presence had taught her. Asia's mind wandered until she fell asleep.

The next morning while getting dressed, Asia realized that adapting to Blac's world and persona was cool and exciting. For this interview, she had to recall what she knew as far as work and professionalism were concerned. With this in mind, she was happy that she didn't throw away her old clothes. She got dressed and coached herself through her thoughts while disciplining her previous actions. The main things that were important for Asia to keep in mind was patience and self-preservation. These were important pieces to the puzzle. Patience was the art of watering a seed and giving it time to grow, knowing that what was meant to be would come to her, as she did gaining access to the company. Self-preservation simply had to do with the access she allowed Dave to have. See, Asia was different. She was innocent, but still sexy. This gave her an advantage; while she probably would try to entice him with sex, or at least the idea of it, Asia realized based on what she knew about him that it may be more beneficial for her to do something out of the ordinary. She was about to be dealing with a wealthy and smart businessman who played in the gutter. While they may have dressed things up elegantly and changed the image, when the materials of the upscale illusion were removed, it was clear that these were pimps, hoes and tricks who used their business connections and power to do and get whatever they wanted. So, Asia had to do something different. Sex was everyone else's game, but Asia's strongest attributes in this situation were her innocence and her seemingly unknowing nature. See, men like Dave like to be painted as if they did something no one else could, and Asia was the good-looking, unnoticed girl who needed to be conquered—at least, that's what Asia hoped Dave would think.

Asia walked into the lobby wearing a black fitted skirt with sheer pantyhose and a soft, pink button-down blouse. Asia pulled her hair back into a ponytail and wore light, natural makeup with clear lip gloss. She walked to the security desk, signed in and headed to the elevator. Asia got onto the elevator with two women who seemed to be paying her a little too much attention. The elevator stopped and Asia was the first to get off. The doors opened and Asia said, "Good day, ladies." The two women had stank looks on their faces as the elevator doors shut. Asia walked down the hall and checked in with the receptionist. The receptionist confirmed Asia's appointment, then walked her to a room. In the room, there was a big wooden table with a glossy finish and black chairs around it. Asia took a seat, and shortly after, a man with a notepad and manila folder walked in and greeted her.

"Good morning. My name is Chris and I will be conducting your interview today. How are you?"

Asia responded, "Morning, Chris," and shook his hand. No special details about him. He was average; to Asia, nothing really stood out about him. He was a tall gentleman who dressed cleanly. He could be in his late 30s, early 40s—a very *average* man. I guess Asia wasn't impressed by him because he wasn't what she was looking for—or *who* she was looking for. However, she still played nice and stayed professional as she smiled and grinned at the man while giving him top-tier answers to his interview questions. While in the interview, Asia couldn't help but wonder if Dave was in the office and, if so, where he was. Asia's thought was interrupted by the receptionist, who came in to interrupt the interview; she seemed extremely worried about something. The receptionist gave Asia a fake smile, leaned into the man who was interviewing Asia and whispered in his ear. The man rolled his eyes and looked at Asia, asking for her forgiveness. He explained that he had something to handle and would be right back. The man stood up, and he and the receptionist left the room. Asia sat there, looking around the room as she patiently waited for the man's return.

Asia wondered what was going on in Blac's world, and if she were to kill Dave, how she would do it. Asia stood up and walked around the room as she snooped in an attempt to get any information she could about the company and its boss. The door opened. Asia turned to see who it was; in front of her stood a bald man who stood at six feet, three inches. He had on a gray suit with a white button-down shirt. Hanging out of the pocket of his suit jacket was a black handkerchief, and on his feet were black dress shoes. The man had beautiful features of a Black king. He had deep dimples and white teeth. Asia was shocked by how handsome this man was and became extremely interested in him.

The man asked, "Sorry, is this room taken?"

Asia said, "I'm interviewing in here."

The man said, "Well, in that case, I'm Davado, but everyone

calls me Big Dave."

Asia said, "My name is Asia. I applied for the temporary assistant position."

Big Dave replied as he shut the door and walked over to the table, "Oh, yeah? You any good? Good help is hard to find. Have a seat, Miss Asia."

Asia sat down. She was confused by how beautiful this man was. He looked like a god, but she knew he was too good to be true. Then, *it* happened. His phone rang and he read someone to filth upon answering. Asia quickly remembered why she was there as he bragged and boasted, making the person on the other end of the line feel as big as a piece of lint. Asia played it cool and became very attentive as he hung up the phone and started asking Asia questions regarding her desired position. Big Dave seemed extremely impressed by Asia's knowledge and answers. While he was closing out his statement, Chris walked into the room. Big Dave stood up and buttoned his jacket, then gave Chris a look with his right eyebrow raised. Chris quickly rushed to the table, apologized for the interruption and sat down.

Big Dave walked towards the door, opened it, and said, "Chris."

Chris said, "Sir."

Big Dave said, "Don't worry about it. I completed the interview. Miss Asia, welcome to the team."

Chris said, "Gre—"

Big Dave said, "Chris, save it. Next time, make sure that you prioritize your day better when you have an interview to conduct. I'm pretty sure we've taken up enough of Miss Asia's time today."
Chris said, "My apologies, Sir, but we had an emergency."

Big Dave said, "That's why we have people in position for that—or should we be interviewing for those positions, too?"

Chis said, "No, sir."

Big Dave said, "Okay. Anyway, Miss Asia, would you care to join me for lunch? It's the least I can do for taking so much of your time."

Asia was surprised. "I guess, if it's no trouble," she said.

Big Dave said, "None at all," and left the office with Asia. They talked as they walked down the hall. When they reached the front security desk, Big Dave let the security guard know that he was going out for lunch and walked Asia to her car. He explained that he had a special parking spot in the parking garage and that she would receive access to it on her first day of work.

Big Dave and Asia then met at a very busy Greek food bistro that appeared to be a hot spot during the lunch hours of the day. Upon arriving, one of the valet guys greeted Asia and told her that her valet parking was taken care of. Asia was slightly impressed and took a mental note. *Okay, Big Dave, with the first-class treatment*, she thought to herself. Asia stood at the door as she watched Big Dave's fine ass take his car to the valet. He smiled and gently put his left hand on the center of Asia's back. Asia knew that this was *not* a business-related lunch—at least, not on his part. They walked into the beautiful restaurant, which had a Tarzan-esque feel to it. There were tree leaves, branches, and black and white zebra patterns painted on the walls. The host greeted Big Dave and escorted Asia and Big Dave to their seats. The pair had a very nice lunch. Asia paid very close attention to Dave during their meal because she wanted to gain as much information about him as possible. The thing that stuck out in Asia's mind was his unapologetic need and desire to speak about himself. Under normal circumstances, that would have been annoying to sit through, but in this situation, she enjoyed him walking her straight through the front door of his life. After plenty of conversation, laughter, and good food, Big Dave offered an invitation for Asia to go dancing with him that evening. Asia quickly accepted—ya girl was dedicated and determined, so she was willing to spend as much time as she could with Big Dave. Patience is the name of the game.

Later that evening, at around 7 p.m., Asia and Big Dave met at a dance club that looked like a dance studio. Asia and Big Dave danced the night away and enjoyed each other's company, participating in Chicago line dances and singing along to tunes.

This was an interesting date for Asia because she did not know most of these dances that he introduced to her, but she definitely wasn't gonna show it, and she definitely wasn't gonna fall behind. Asia kept up with Big Dave quite well and they laughed a lot as they danced. This seemed like a real date, and the lines began to blur in Asia's eyes. These lines needed to blur so that Asia could be free and let her hair down while retaining anything that she could and making him become more interested in her. The time began to get late, so they said their goodnights and went their separate ways. Over the next several days, Asia and Big Dave spent a lot of time together, from lunches to evenings out on the town. Big Dave was married, though, so this was interesting. Asia didn't know how he made time for her, but he did. She figured that the saying, "You make time for what you want," applied to this. Big Dave became very fond of Asia and started doing things that showed his openness with her, and he tended to let his guard down a lot now. On their first lunch date, Big Dave carried a pistol on his waist that he did not hide from the rest of the world because he had a permit to legally carry a gun. But as he and Asia became closer, the pistol became less and less visible. Big Dave had become so comfortable that he didn't feel the need to make it visual when he would go places with her. Asia felt like this meant that he didn't feel threatened. He was comfortable, and this was good for Asia. Friday morning came—the morning that everybody had anticipated because a group of 100 businessmen who were known to play were supposed to be coming into town for a convention. Now, this was the biggest event of the month, which caused the most commotion.

Earlier, Big Dave had spoken about putting together a stable of girls to satisfy all of the elite guys, but Asia had thrown off his focus. So, instead of Big Dave paying attention to Blac and the women of leisure, he asked Asia to go away with him for the weekend. She knew that this would indirectly help Blac, whether she needed it or not, so she accepted Big Dave's offer. Asia and Big Dave went away to a cabin in the country and spent the whole weekend there. Asia displayed a more mature and sensual side of herself that was nurtured by the amount of love and affection that she had seen throughout her life, whether through movies, TV, or even her parents. She used her ability to feel and communicate without using words to make love to Big Dave all weekend—yes, *all* weekend. They enjoyed intimate moments and made lots of love as they got to know each other, and they spent a lot of time with each other. This was an extremely intimate encounter for Asia because she had never spent that much time on one person who she knew would eventually disappear from her life.

This also spoke volumes about Asia's focus and her determination to conquer her opponent. Asia couldn't help but wonder what his wife was thinking and where she thought he was. She guessed that Dave was used to doing whatever he wanted and that his wife simply accepted it. Asia believed that she had now gathered enough information to know just how to make her next move. The weekend came to an end; it was now time for Asia to end this fairytale and start the nightmare—going back to reality. Asia and Big Dave walked to their cars to say their goodbyes. Big Dave expressed the amount of enjoyment and happiness he had experienced over the last couple of days. He compared the feeling to being complete and fulfilled, and spoke about how grateful he was. Big Dave explained to Asia that he didn't want the experience to end and that he was excited to build a future with her. Asia smiled and received what he was saying, while in her mind doubting everything as she realized that it was all a game she wasn't buying. It was a game to her because not only was he married, but he was also a self-centered and arrogant asshole and it showed. Asia kissed Big Dave on the cheek, thanked him for a wonderful weekend and went on with her day.

Monday morning marked the beginning of the end. Asia went to the parking garage where Big Dave was parked. Asia arrived at about 9 a.m. because she knew that Big Dave would already be there since he liked to get his day started early. Big Dave drove a red Ferrari with red chrome rims; he would usually cover his car so that no one could touch it and security would keep an eye on it. Asia set off the emergency alarm in the parking lot, which distracted the security guard. The guard went to locate the blaring alarm and shut it off. As the security guard got up to shut off the alarm, Asia used the parking lot access code that Chris had sent her in an email. She drove until she spotted Big Dave's car and parked across from it. Asia got out of the car wearing a black bodysuit and a black full-face mask with a black bag in her hand. She slid around the perimeter of Big Dave's car and quickly placed a black box under it. After she finished, she stood in the elevator where she quickly removed her bodysuit and replaced it with a black, button-down, tight-fitting dress.

She pulled her hair out of her ponytail, shook it for volume, put on her pumps and threw a purple scarf around the bag she was carrying. She walked into the coffee shop and floated to a open table. Now, Asia knew that Big Dave would be leaving out of the office at around 11 a.m. to come meet her for lunch. Big Dave texted Asia to confirm the lunch date, but she didn't respond. He became frantic and continued to send her back-to-back text messages, but received no response. Big Dave decided that he was going to go to lunch anyway, with the hope that Asia was busy with something else at the moment and would just meet him there. When Big Dave got into his car, he stopped at the security post to let him know that he was heading out for lunch. Asia sat in the coffee shop downstairs and watched Big Dave as he let down the top of his convertible and put on his glasses while bopping his head to the music that came out of his stereo. Asia started the timer for the bomb. Big Dave reached the corner of the street and in seconds, his car blew up. People began running and the only audible sound was that of sirens.

CHAPTER 7
SHORT AND SWEET

Somewhere across town, Smalls was with Blac, brainstorming for a charity event that they were planning together. Her phone rang and she answered it. She had a short conversation with someone and became frantic as she got off the phone.

Smalls said, "Blac, listen. The streets just got real."

Blac looked at Smalls and said, "Look, I don't have time for this. I got stuff I need to be doing. We need to figure it out and get on with our day."

Smalls said, "No, Blac. Somebody just blew up Davado car."

Blac looked at Smalls and said, "What?"

Smalls said, "You heard me—somebody just blew up Big Dave's car. I don't know what he did but he definitely went up in flames. That's probably why he wasn't tripping on you. He had other stuff going on."

Bo walked in and said, "What y'all got going on?"

Blac said, "Working, getting this event together. Oh, by the way, somebody bombed Dave."

Bo said, "Get out of here. How you know?!"

Blac said, "Smalls just got word a couple of minutes ago." Bo said, "That's crazy, but he was wild, so it was bound to happen one way or another."

Blac looked at Bo and said, "That's a damn shame, but you know how it go. You live by the sword, you die by the sword. Whoever it was ain't wanna leave nothing for the family."

Bo said, "Sad."

Blac said, "Anyways, let's wrap this up. I got a lot of stuff I gotta do today."

Blac walked out to her car, where she was greeted by her driver. Her driver opened the door for her. Inside, she picked up her phone to make a phone call. Asia was across town, sitting in the lobby of the coffee shop that she had damn near become a resident of by now. She answered her phone. "Hello," said Asia.

Blac said, "Kaboom. Well, hello, boss lady."

Asia smirked, gave a small laugh and said, "Well, hello, ma'am. How are you? Sorry I been distant; I been occupied a bit." Blac said, "Well, occupied is good, and I couldn't be any better. How are you?"

Asia said, "I'm just peachy."

Blac said, "Well, everybody ain't able. Some people blow up before they make it to the top."

Asia started laughing and said, "Well, at least you know. Some things just get blown out of proportion."

Blac nodded her head up and down and said, "OK, I get it. Message received. When can you meet me?"

Asia said, "I can meet you this evening. I like 8, at the house."

Blac said, "I'll beat you there."

Asia said, "I'll meet you there."

They both hung up. Blac looked at her phone and, in a low tone, said to herself, "This could work." On the other end of the phone, Asia breathed a sigh of relief. This was the feeling of fulfillment and pleasure as it was now noted that Asia could take initiative and move in a mature and professional manner. Somehow, since she felt like she had earned Blac's appreciation or honor, she was ready to claim her spot in the family.

Asia walked through the house, entering Blac's room.

Blac said, "Sit down, no one else is here. It's just me. Sit down. Sit."

Asia sat on the chair that was across from Blac's bed. On the table was a pile of money. Asia had never seen that much money in her life, but she kept her composure because she didn't want to make Blac doubt her feelings about her. Blac sat on the bed in front of Asia and the table and said, "So, how much do I owe you?" Asia said, "This was on the house. I needed to prove a point, so I did."

Blac said, "You did, but there are certain necessities when you accomplish that type of task because there are things that come with that territory that would make it worth it or not. You need to learn your worth. I don't care what point you were trying to prove—you did a job, and you deserve what comes to you with that job. You gon' take the negative things that come with it, so it's expected that you accept the positive, too. It's called balance. So, what do you think is appropriate for that?"

Asia put her hand on her chin, looked into the sky and said, "Maybe $50,000."

Blac laughed and said, "Girllll, you *cheap*! I like cheap, but you wrong. You put so much into that. I haven't seen you in a couple of days, so I know you've been sitting on that man for at least a week at the minimum. So, let me give you some advice: This was a lick or a trick, no matter how you look at it. When you claim your price, you have to take all of those things into consideration. Did you have sex with him?"

Asia said, "Do it matter?"

Blac said, "Yes. Listen, it's not my business—that's your body, do what you want. But I do wanna let you know that that's a part of your pricing. There's time and patience, which you should be charging top price for since you ain't got none. Anything that you put effort into during the process, you charge for, period. So, it's important to claim your price and make sure it's worth what you put in. I'ma give you $150,000."

Asia's eyes got really big.

Blac said, "Don't mention it. Any problem that may come with that situation or anything I hear that may come to you, I'll take care of it. The major thing about it is that when you do jobs, no matter who you doing them for, you always claim your price and make sure that the price they pay you is worth the time and effort you put into it. Don't ever forget that."

Blac put the money into a duffel bag and gave it to Asia. Blac said, "Lay low for a couple of days. It's definitely gonna be spooky around here, but you'll be fine if you stay out the way."

Asia thanked Blac and took mental notes of what she said about claiming her price and staying out the way. Asia did this oh so well. She literally became Blac's favorite person who no one ever saw. This was beneficial for both Blac and Asia. With Asia playing this position, the dynamic between her and Blac flourished. They developed a close love and loyalty for each other that was often tested, but most of the obstacles they overcame together strengthened their bond and made them stronger as individuals. While one would argue that Blac didn't need the assistance, actions showed that Asia didn't, either—just guidance. In their own way, they needed each other.

CHAPTER 8
BECOMING BLAC/SEX SELLS

Cars passed on a busy street while four little girls played on the sidewalk. One of the little girls took a small rock and rolled it up the street until it stopped. The same little girl began hopping on the sidewalk, avoiding the area where the rock stopped while the other three little girls watched. They were playing hopscotch. The girls didn't have chalk or money to buy any. Instead, they made the hopscotch board by using the rocks and scratching them against the pavement until the hopscotch pattern appeared.

"Olivia!" yelled a woman who was hanging out of one of the apartment windows.

All four of the girls stopped and looked up to see that Olivia's, one of the little girls who was playing hopscotch, mom was calling her in for dinner. These little girls would get together after school on weekday afternoons and on weekends. All of these girls' mothers knew each other because they lived in the same area and their children played and went to school together.

"OK, Mom, I'm coming," Olivia shouted back.

She handed the rock over to another little girl, who looked up at the woman in the window and said, "Hey, Miss Susie."

Miss Susie looked at her and said, "Hey, Barbe! You need to get in the house and go wake your mom up because it's almost time for her to get up and it's starting to get late."

The little girl, Barbe, put the rock down and ran upstairs to her apartment to wake up her mom. Barbe would grow up to be Blac. Blac was very outspoken and independent, even as a young woman. She had to be, because her mom was a bar owner who would stay out all night and then sleep all day. Barbe was the oldest of three children. She had two younger brothers, who would grow up to be street gangsters just as they were taught to. Barbe walked into the house, where her two brothers were sitting in the living room playing a video game.

Barbe told them to wash their hands and get ready for dinner because she had to figure out something to make as she looked in the refrigerator. She closed the refrigerator door, headed out of the kitchen and back into the living room. She looked at one of her brothers and said, "Hey, Joseph, is Mommy awake?"

Sammy, Blac's youngest brother, was the baby of the family and the highlight of her mother's life. Sammy looked at Barbe and said, "I don't know. Go see."

Barbe looked at him with her two French braids to the back of her head. She said, "I can't stand you. I'ma beat you up when I get out of Mommy's room."

Sammy looked at Barbe and said, "If you hit me, I'm telling Mama."

Blac looked at Sammy and said, "Boy, I *am* Mama," as she walked through the living room to go to her mom's room. She knocked on the door because she didn't want to disturb her if she was in the room with somebody. Her mother did not respond or say anything, so that's what let her know that no one else was in the room. Barbe, better known as young Blac, opened the door and found Mama asleep and exposed. As she entered the room, Barbe pulled the curtain open, exposing the streetlight and sun that had mixed together because it had started to get late and night was arriving. After bringing some light into the dark room, she stood next to her mom's nightstand and grabbed the glass of water that was now room temperature due to sitting as long as it had.

Barbe's mother closed her eyes tightly and said a long, "Ummm," as she stretched out and exposed her boobs to her daughter, who seemed to have disturbed a good sleep.

Barbe's mom said, "Girl, what do you want? I'm tired, Barbe." Barbe said, "Mama, it's time to get up; it's almost time to open the bar."

Her mother asked, "What time is it?" as she reached for the glass of water in Barbe's hand.

Barbe said, "Mama, it's almost 7."

Her mother grunted, grabbed her silk robe and sat at the edge of her bed with her feet touching the ground. Sluggishly, she put her arms through the sleeves of the robe to cover herself and tidied up a bit as she sat up in her bed and drank more of the water that her baby girl had given her. Barbe sat at the edge of the bed and asked her mother if she needed anything.

Her mother said, "No, I'm fine. I just got a slight headache, but I'll be OK."

Barbe said, "Well, I'm gonna make Joseph and Sammy some dinner. Do you want some?"

Her mother said, "No, honey, I don't want any, but thank you for taking care of your brothers. You've always taken really good care of your brothers. That's an awesome thing. That's what big girls do." Her mom smiled at her and looked at her phone to see if anybody had called her while she was asleep. Barbe got up, walked out the room and went to go feed her brothers. While Barbe and her brothers sat in front of the TV watching cartoons and eating dinner, her mother emerged from her room. This was not the same woman who was tore up and exposed waking up from a drunken night. This woman wore a fur coat and a tight-fitting blue dress, with her hair straightened and flowing down her back. Her makeup was flawless and she had on diamond jewelry.

Barbe's mom stood in the hall and said, "Y'all are going to go brain-dead watching TV."

Sammy, the youngest brother, said, "No, ma'am, we not."

Barbe's mom looked at him and said, "What did I say?"

Sammy said, "Sorry, Mom."

Barbe looked up at her mother, who was looking beautiful as she always did, and said, "Mom, are you headed out?"

The woman looked at her young daughter, shaking her head and rolling her eyes. "Yes, I'm headed to the crazy place with the crazy people," she said. "Just call me if you need anything and I'll make sure you get it. You know the rules, you know what to do. Barbe make sure Sammy and Joseph are in bed by 10."

Barbe agreed to see to her brothers getting to bed. Barbe also kissed her mother and told her to have a good night as her mother walked away in her red leather shoes. Barbe's mother walked out the door, sighing. She looked back at Barbe with a long face and said, "Boy, I don't wanna go. I wish I could just give you the keys to the bar and let you open it up and run it so I could stay here and watch cartoons."

Blac laughed and kissed her mom goodnight again as she slammed the door and headed into the night. The strangest thing about that situation was that eventually, that's exactly what ended up happening. You wouldn't see Barbe's mom in the house watching cartoons, but she definitely allowed Barbe to have input in and power in the bar in ways one wouldn't believe as she became older. Barbe was basically raised in the bar and did everything she could to help out, from running errands to mopping, washing dishes and sweeping. By the time Barbe turned 14, she would get dressed and sit at the bar with her mom. Barbe's mother filled the neighborhood guys up with drinks and drugs and allowed them to flirt with Barbe and buy her drinks all night. Barbe was extremely good-looking and her natural figure filled out at a young age, so she could get whatever she wanted. Patrons of the bar had hopes of getting Barbe drunk enough to leave with them, but she and her mother had a system. Her mother would have a clear bottle of what they claimed was tequila, and every time a man would offer to buy Barbe a drink, she would charge him the fee for tequila and pour the nonalcoholic liquid into a glass for Barbe. Barbe and her mom would split the profit. So, by the end of the night, Barbe would be going home with a small profit, and as she got older, the profit became bigger.

This type of atmosphere and these activities helped baby girl Barbe to become a form of entertainment and outlet for the men who sought companionship outside of their homes. Even though Barbe may have known their wives and children, she still stuck to the plan. Plus, it wasn't personal—it was business and everyone knew it. One night while at the bar, a man got so wasted that he gave Barbe his wallet. Barbe went through the wallet, took out all of the cash and left the wallet on the bar as she would do any other man that was foolish enough to get that drunk. The next night, the man returned to the bar, but he wasn't there to drink and socialize. He was there to look for the little Barbie doll who took his cash in his wallet. When he got there, Barbe's mom was behind the bar. She watched the old man, who came in upset and soberer than a nun at Easter Mass.

Barbe's mom hand washed a glass with a cigarette in her mouth, looked at the man standing by the door and said, "Hey, handsome. You back for round two?"

He said, "No, I ain't here for no round two. I'm looking for that little girl of yours who robbed me."

She looked at him and said, "Ain't no little girl of mine robbed you! My daughter ain't rob nobody."

The man looked at her and said, "Yes, she did, and I'm a kill 'er."

Barbe's mom said, "Shut up, you drunk fool. You ain't gon' kill nobody. And if you knew anything about me, even if you killed people, you would know that you weren't gon' touch my baby. Don't be upset that you got caught with your pants down and now you want some revenge for what you think happened."

Beautiful Barbe walked out of the billiards area wearing a black dress with black lipstick and black eyeshadow, her hair curled and laid to one side.

The man shouted across the room at the black beauty that had arrived, "Hey, little girl!"

Barbe looked at the man and said, "Do I even know you?" The man stood in front of Barbe and said, "Little girl, you don't know me, but you sure spent my money. You *do* know me from last night. I was in here getting filled up by your mama, and she probably put something in my drink. When I got home, I looked in my wallet and all of the cash was gone."

Barbe looked at him and said, "Well, you must have spent it at the bar. I don't keep tabs on drunk people and what they spend."

He looked at her and said, "People come down here after a long day's work to unwind and relax, and you get them out of their minds to rob them."

Barbe said, "I ain't rob nobody, and sir, if you wanna relax in comfort, do it at home. You never get *that* out of your mind at a public place like this—look around! It's pimps, hoes and hustlers everywhere. That's dangerous, especially for you."

The man's eyes bulged really big and he said, "Who taught you to speak in that tone, you evil little girl? I bet your heart is black and made of coal."

Barbie responded, "Yup. It's as black as Alaska during their blackout season. You see the color." She rolled her eyes and walked away from the upset man.

So, there you have it—that's where she got the name Blac. After that encounter, everybody at Blac's mom's bar would acknowledge her as Blac. No one called her Barbe anymore; most people didn't even know that was her name unless they were her childhood friends or went to school with her. Even the kids from school knew not to call her Barbe outside of the classroom anytime Blac saw them or they saw her. They were instructed to call her Blac. This became such a common nickname that her little brothers even got into the habit of using it. Barbe was OK with being called Blac because as welcoming and fun as she was, in a split second, she could change, and everything would get dark and glamorous. While black was a sexy color and what she also thought to be a sexy name, it came with a negative notion. With her reputation for helping her mother drug and rob the men at the bar once they were drunk, Blac took pride in her name and felt that it gave her a sense of power. The nickname Blac stuck with her throughout her whole life.

Blac was an extremely no-nonsense and taken young woman from her childhood up into her adulthood. Blac would do whatever was necessary to get her money, whether it was rob, steal or cheat. She figured out a way to get money and stay out of her mom's pockets. Her mother wasn't evil, but she still got drunk all night and slept all day. Even as Blac became a teenager and then an adult, Blac still made it her business to go to her mother's room to medicate her and do what she needed to do to help her feel better so that she could open up the bar every night. Blac played more of a motherly figure to her younger brothers and made sure that they did what they were supposed to do as far as staying in school and getting their schoolwork done. While most of Blac's friends and classmates had parents who were there for them to, as Blac saw it, hold their hands, she didn't have that same luxury.

She taught herself most of the morals and standards that she had, which didn't quite fit into the street and night lifestyle. Her mother taught her discipline by having her watch the wrong ways of doing things. Blac knew that in order to be any type of example and help guide the boys, she had to have a good balance, and she did just that. She would watch documentaries and read books about famous philosophers and businessmen and apply them to her life. As complicated as it was to try to keep the boys out of trouble, she did her best. Unfortunately, when you are a little Black boy growing up around poverty and sometimes very bad things, you adapt to your surroundings. While Joseph got in trouble at a very early age, he was able to leave and experience a different type of life. Joseph left to go live with Blac's grandparents when he was 13.

Sammy and Blac stayed with their mother and both got into the street business. Sammy was a bad little boy who was known for beating people up until he picked up a job for one of the neighborhood crews. Blac was devastated, but she did everything she could do to protect her brother and keep him out of as much trouble as she could, but he was growing up and she couldn't keep much of a handle on him. Blac wasn't an angel, and she didn't pretend to be one, either. Blac prided herself on taking an authentic and realistic approach about her life. She worked in the streets as well, but she didn't sell drugs, nor did she consider herself a killer. Simply put, she was a sex worker. Blac already knew a little bit about men. Blac knew that when liquor and sexy women were involved, she could pretty much get any horny fool. Blac used this to her advantage. She had created a very elite clientele of men that would come into town, come to the bar and look for her. She started doing this at the age of 15 and she was pretty successful.

Blac was popular in her neighborhood, and amongst the conversation of the elite, these men would bring money and gifts to her mom just so she could pass the message along to Blac that they were looking for her. Blac's mother was money-driven and it showed, so she would allow them access to her daughter. These men would come to Blac's mom and set up times when they could come and meet Blac. Blac was sexy, but she was mean, and that's what men seemed to like about her. She had always been business oriented and did not take any shortcuts or negotiations when it came down to her time. When Blac was six years old, her father was killed in a drive-by shooting. She never recovered from this because she watched it from the window of her apartment. Her father had been on his way to visit her and her younger brothers. At the time, baby brother Sammy was only six months old, and he and Blac smiled and cheered their dad on as he approached the front door of the apartment. When he got to the door, a car with three men and automatic weapons inside shot at him. Blac's dad was shot twice in the back and once in the back of his head. Blac never fully recovered from this but accepted the fact that she had an angel who was always there with her, protecting her. At least, that's what her mother would tell her when she would ask questions about her father.

Blac's mother taught her everything she could about being sexy and being a woman, but there were certain things that Blac's mother couldn't teach her because although she was a successful bar owner, she was not business-oriented. The bar was basically run by the gangsters and pimps because her mother would borrow money from them that she would later owe. So, she was basically a worker in her own business. Blac watched this happen in her early years of being an escort and promised herself that she would never be that way. She wanted to own everything that she had because in her mind, if she didn't work for herself, she would end up working for somebody else. So, Blac did just that. She worked for herself and created a good life for herself; she eventually, at the age of 17, moved out of her mom's small two-bedroom apartment and got her own in a more elite area of the city. She moved to the nicer part of town because that was where the type of clientele she wanted to attract lived. Blac didn't want to attract pimps and drug users. She wanted to attract businessmen and mobsters who were high-ranking. There's something about the power of the mind and tongue, because there would come a time where she would have to address those types of people with her chest. She had always been friendly with the ladies and would usually bring two or three with her when she had big licks to handle and would travel out of town. Blac and her girls became a hot commodity. All of the elite businessmen and mobsters wanted a piece of Blac.

While most couldn't afford her time, it didn't stop the lingering desire and urge that she would leave with them. Those back at her mother's bar knew that they couldn't buy her a drink, so they were OK with just listening to her stories, but the ones who could afford time with Blac definitely paid the fee and enjoyed every moment of it. Blac and her girls would receive random gifts and perks of the life they lived, such as jewelry, clothes, shopping sprees, cars, shoes and all-expenses-paid trips. Blac pretty much had a handle on this life she had created and on this new elite group of women she surrounded herself with. As perfect as it may seem, Blac and her girls were steadily targeted by the lower-level pimps and nightshift neighborhood cops. Blac was always honest and realistic about the trouble that came with her lifestyle; she believed this was what made her so credible and easy for girls to talk to. This type of trouble became a routine and contributed to the way she saw her luck. She held a philosophy that, for every three good days, she would have to have one bad day in order to balance things out. This kept her optimistic and welcoming toward her mishaps, from her numerous arrests and troubles with the guys to the many times she was robbed. She accepted it all because the experiences molded her and kept her relevant in conversation. She didn't mind people talking badly about her—at least they were talking. Blac had a good and soft heart but a tough and cold exterior. Her Uncle Prince could be thanked for that.

Uncle Prince was the brother of Blac's father. Uncle Prince moved into the neighborhood where Blac's father got killed in order to watch over her mother and her two younger brothers. Blac enjoyed the comfort of knowing that Uncle Prince was always around. Blac also enjoyed talking to and following Uncle Prince. Uncle Prince would take Blac with him on different trips that he would go on to handle different types of business affairs. So, by the age of 10, Blac knew all of the big mobsters and gangsters in the neighborhood. This ultimately helped Blac growing up, and in her business, Uncle Prince also taught her how to gamble, shoot guns and take things that didn't belong to her. While these things weren't Blac's fortes or things that she wanted to do, she sure had the tools and resources to get them done. When Uncle Prince learned about her getting into his lifestyle, he had a serious conversation with her in which he let her know that she was entering a dangerous world where she would need lots of protection. He decided to keep a close eye on her, whether she was in the neighborhood or in the city's elite areas. Uncle Prince never made his presence known, but he made everybody know that Blac was his niece and that messing with her would result in the killing of one's whole family. Uncle Prince wasn't someone who was played with. He worked very closely with the mob and people knew that he didn't have any loyalty to anyone in the neighborhood because the only person who he could have loyalty to was already dead. Uncle Prince was a very handsome man, but he was very dark and cold. He showed no emotion at all, not even to Blac. Sometimes, she would be so confused and uncomfortable during conversations because he would be very stern and have hard conversations with her.

This taught her how to be stern and be cold during matters of life and death. Uncle Prince ran multiple businesses and made a lot of money. He was not forgiving—"once you cross me, you've lost me." That's what he would say to warn people of the harsh and stern way he would treat others who dealt with him, to let them know not to challenge him. While he was OK with being the Boogie Man of the streets, he experienced some trauma that haunted and hurt him—like his little niece running around with pimps and hoes.

Uncle Prince never forgave Blac's mom for allowing her around that lifestyle and pimping her into it. In Uncle Prince's eyes, Blac's mother was a disgrace. Instead of giving Blac the guidance to get away and be something different like Joseph, he felt that her mom gave her the tools she *wanted* her to have to get into the lifestyle she was now a part of. He didn't show love and appreciation to her for being the mother of his niece and nephews. Uncle Prince looked at her as a woman who did nothing but get drunk and sleep all day and night—that's what he would say to her when they would get into arguments.

Uncle Prince was well-connected and well-respected and would usually help her when she had really bad blood with the gangsters and pimps. Due to bad debt and deals, they would pretty much run over life and her business. Blac's mom was good at taking their abuse, especially when she was wrong, but like most people, she had her limits to what she could endure as well. When these moments came, Uncle Prince would pop up and Blac's mom would feel a sense of relief. On another note, it was strange how he would just *know* when things weren't right with her. It was as if he felt it in his spirit, but he probably just had one of the nosy ladies in the neighborhood let him know when things were dangerous between his sister-in-law and the guys. Uncle Prince was a hoe like that, so it wouldn't be a surprise if he did. Uncle Prince didn't deal with the boys as much because he couldn't deal with the way they looked. This was because they reminded him too much of his dead brother. When he would speak to them, he would look off to the side, not making much eye contact. Uncle Prince still loved both of his nephews very much, but the thought or visual of them just hurt him too much, especially considering that his brother was not a street guy. Blac came up in an unstable, fast and dangerous atmosphere, which taught her to depend on herself and take care of those who couldn't take care of themselves. The emotions she experienced left a long-lasting impression on her and impacted how she took on the world—but good luck getting Blac Monroe to admit these things.

CHAPTER 9
FRENCH BENEFITS/FRENCH KISSES

A live jazz band played and sang in a room that was decorated with black, gold and silver. The room had big balloon arches and decorations throughout. There were many men and women walking around in tuxedos and dress shirts with ties, serving food and champagne to the people who sat at the tables. On a balcony above the band was really long table that stretched from one side of the room to the other. The band took their seats on the stage, where Blac and her entourage of people could be seen.

The lead singer of the band stood, stole the microphone and said, "Everybody, quiet down. Blac wants to give a toast," then sat down.

The beautiful Blac, in her long, gold custom silk Chanel dress, held up a glass. She wore a diamond choker, a custom Rolex watch, diamond bracelets on both wrists and a very big ring on her left ring finger.

Blac said, "Good evening, everyone. Again, I wanna thank everyone for coming to celebrate my life and the success of our company. We have had a very successful couple of years, and none of it would be possible without the people who help run it. First, I wanna thank Angelica, my assistant, my notepad, my cell phone, my therapist, my punching bag—my everything, pretty much. You have worked for me for about eight years now, and I don't believe that I would be able to do all the things that I'm able to do without you. Thank you for tolerating me and for accepting everything that comes with me—the good, the bad and the ugly. Bo, as much as you may get on my last nerve at times, you serve your purpose. Thank you for always protecting us and making sure that everybody who encounters us is gentle, genuine, warm and welcoming. You are always there standing at attention, ready to destroy anything that comes in our way, and for that, I am more than grateful. My Nicole, the light of my room, the most bubbly, no-nonsense-taking, Sour Patch, happy-now-but-will-cry-in-five-minutes little girl I've ever met in my life—excuse me, young woman, because I met you as a little girl. Now, you're flourishing to be a very successful and independent woman—thanks to me, of course. But nevertheless, if you didn't have it in you, it wouldn't be possible. You have brought me some jews, and you have brought me some rocks, but nevertheless, you're always trying to figure out a way to bring the family to the top, and for that, I will always be in debt to you, my love.

While everybody in this room is important, I saved my best for last. This young woman was a problem from the day I met her. Not only did she almost make me crash my car the first time I seen her, she definitely was everlasting from the first time I ever invited her to one of the houses. If you know what I'm saying, then you know who I'm talking about: my Asia. Asia has always been my shadow and protégé since the day she came into my life. I am very grateful for you. I appreciate you for carrying the torch, and I am ecstatic to see what your future has in store, because this is just the beginning.

Everyone followed Blac in raising their glasses, and Blac said, "To success." The room said, "To success." Blac attempted to take a drink from her glass, stopped and said, "Oh, wait. Let's not forget the finest and most important person on Earth."

Nicole looked at Asia and rolled her eyes. Blac said, "My husband, my love, my protector, my everything. No, he couldn't be here tonight because, as you know, he's too busy 'running the world' like he always says. But he definitely gave me my birthday gift last night *and* this morning, and trust me, every moment was worth the wait."

Nicole looked at Blac and said, "Ew."

Blac laughed and said, "Now, child. You don't be hatin'!"

Nicole said, "Not at all."

Blac and the rest of the room raised their glasses, and Blac said, "Yes, to my Mr. Charlie."

Bo raised his glass and started to make barking noises. Blac's eyes got really big. She looked at him and said, "Boy, is you crazy?"

Bo said, "Sorry, I was just trying to live a little."

Nicole said, "Chill out, Blac. Let that man live," and in her loudest, squeakiest voice yelled, "HAPPY BIRTHDAY, BLAC!"

Blac shook her head, raised her glass higher and said, "I hate y'all. The club laughed and Blac gulped down her glass of champagne. She said, "Everybody, let's party."

So that's what they did; this was a good night for everyone. Blac got to do what she did best—be the center of attention—while entertaining her guests. She wouldn't have it any other way. Business was good and the family seemed to be happy; it seemed like the ideal birthday gift, considering what she had been working for all her life. This seemed like a gutter fairy tale where the bad guys disappeared and the people who were rough around the edges with good intentions sparkled like some sexy diamonds. That's the thing about the top spot. It's never a comfortable position because you never know what can happen next. You just never know where destiny and obstacles are hiding. The unfortunate truth is that sometimes, before we can realize or see it coming, it's already happening, and we just gotta do what we know.

Asia entered a very busy and tall building in the business district of the city's downtown area. The scenery was comparable to classic New York, but the atmosphere was slowed down and relaxed. She walked on the marble floors of this seemingly well-kept building as her shoes made music with her steps. She stopped in front of a silver, mirror-like elevator door and it opened.

She entered the elevator wearing a long black coat with patent leather black shoes, black stockings and a black choker necklace with matching earrings and a matching bracelet. she kept catching the attention of a man who appeared to be accompanied by a slender, well-put-together, younger Asian woman who was staring at her breasts and bottom. Asia looked at the man through her black glasses; he looked straight ahead and cleared his throat. *Ding!* The elevator stopped. Asia slowly exited the elevator, turned around, stopped at the door and blew the man a kiss. The woman gasped and slapped the soul out of the man before the elevator door closed.

Chaos surrounded Asia as she heard phones ringing and people chatting. She walked down a long hall that had offices on one side and big, beautiful glass windows on the other side. These windows allowed one to see a beautiful city if they dared to stand in front of them and look down. A young woman speed-walked for about 10 feet, then… A voice yelled, "ASIA!"

Asia turned around and replied with a lengthy, "Yesss?"

"Well, good morning. How nice of you to join us for our meeting. You are always so graciously late whenever you show up for one."

Asia responded with, "Good morning. do you want to make it to lunch? If so, I suggest strongly you answer the phone or book an appointment and leave me to my long walk to the dungeon." Angelica responded, "Maybe I'll do just that. But for your information, she's gonna kill you! Man, I wish I could come at my leisure like you, ol' glamorous one."

Angelica and Asia stopped walking. Asia turned to look at angelica and said, "Oh, Angelica, my dear, sweet, pesterous, bored human of this wonderful world, I have not had my morning regimen that allows me to stomach such sarcasm and underlying admiration that one would mistake for jealousy." She put her pointer finger up and continued, "So, I suggest that you leave me be, or I'll walk into this office and tell your boss that you are not interested in a promotion. You don't want that, do you?" Asia raised her eyebrow. Angelica turned her back to Asia and returned to her desk. Asia walked to angelica's desk, leaned into her and whispered, "I didn't think so!" she walked closer to the door catty-cornered to Angelica's desk, then loudly said, "Good day, Angelica!" and left Angelica to simmer in her words.

Asia opened the office door. A woman spoke on the phone

within the office and said, "Relax, Phil. You will be just fine, but I can't be everywhere! If that was the case, I wouldn't need you!" laughing, she continued, "Phil, I have to go. Hollywood has showed up to put me out of my misery… no, no, no! Phil, I have to go! sir, figure it out!" She hung up the phone.

Asia said, "Good morning, Blac."

The lady in the office said, "Well, well, well, if it isn't the stars and the moon itself! Good morning, royalty! What do I owe this visit? Because I know you don't attend meetings! So, Asia, why are you here?"

Asia responded, "Don't harass me. You know why I'm here and what I want!"

"Lonely at the top, huh?" said Blac.

Asia responded, "Well, everybody can't have a Charlie and live a fairytale life like you, ma'am."

Blac said, "Don't patronize me. We both know my life is far from perfect and I'd much rather live the life I have created for others, but instead, I was captured by a selfish, possessive shark with painful lockjaw."

Asia said, "Cry me a river. You have a sick infatuation for torture and the idea of pain excites you, so I know you have ways around his grip."

Blac laughed and responded, "You know me so well.

Anyways, my dear, I may have something that might excite you, but

I won't know until after tonight!"

Asia said, "TONIGHT?"

Blac said, "Yes, ma'am! Tonight, I have a meeting, and if they don't bring music to my ears, then you will get your fix!"

Asia yelled, "Blac! I can't wait 'til tonight!"

Angelica burst into the office and said, "Everything OK in here?"

Blac responded, "Giiirrrlll, yo' skirt must be too tight or you must be in a bad mental trance to bust in my door like that. And if it wasn't, what were you gonna do?"

Asia sarcastically agreed, "Yeah, Angelica, what exactly was you gonna do?"

Blac said, "Angelica, close it!" Angelica closed the door. Blac waited until the door was completely closed, walked behind Asia and said, "You listen to me. The next time you allow your emotions to get that much control of you… you won't forget it! Don't *ever* raise your voice in my place of business."

Asia interrupted, "But you don't understand. I need this." Blac said, "You *need* this? What is wrong with you? You have clearly forgotten the reasons for that part of the plan to be executed when necessary and *only* then. So, now, you come in here yelling and throwing a fit because you have some high or get some excitement off of playing God!"

Asia said, "If I'm God, you're the law."

Blac said, "Don't you dare drag me into this sick mental game that you play with yourself to get you through. The difference is that I make sacrifices and hard decisions based on the greater good and the protection of the people around me."

Asia interjected, "And I don't?"

Blac said, "You do your part and you do it well, but the difference between you and me is that I follow rules and guidelines, and I don't live my work!"

Asia said, "What do you expect me to do? It's not all houses on the hill and horses in the stable when you're at the top of the hit list."

Blac said, "Lawd, please don't give me your tears today. I can't take it. Listen, I have always taught all of you that when walking through the storm, you have to be focused, and in the world we live in, you have to have tunnel vision. And don't expect light from the dark—you have to create your own light. And in Hollywood, you have to bring the lights, camera and paparazzi and don't give up 'til you have overcome the obstacles on your journey and that's it! So, go read a book, knit a scarf, I don't know. Just occupy your time and don't let this world consume you, 'cause when we dead or under the jail, someone else will be running it, and all we will be is a memory.

Don't let it consume you! Run, now... you could use a nap."

Asia said, "I am not sleepy."

Blac said, "Well, get you something to eat."

Asia said, "OK, I am going! Oh, Blac, by the way, we won't be memories. We'll be glamorous horror stories." She smirked and pointed her pointer finger at Blac.

While sitting at her desk, Blac smiled, nodded her head up and down and said, "Baby... it may not be a house on the hill, but it's certainly a mansion on acres with foreigns in the garage. Now, shut my door. Thank you, ma'am." She picked up her pen and started writing on her paper.

Asia smiled, grabbed the door handle, closed the door and left.

CHAPTER 10
THE BLACK SILHOUETTE/HIP SWINGER

Blac and four other gentlemen were sitting at a round table in the front of the club. This club was called The Black Silhouette. It was the hangout spot for the elite amongst the nightlife and the underworld. This was a place where all the mobsters, hoes, pimps, functional drug addicts and elites in politics and any other powerful industries would meet up. This was not the place where the working class or the poor would hang out; this place was very expensive to enter and it cost even more to get a table. Blac and her other four comrades had a table right in the front, where Blac could have the perfect view of the band. This was the most expensive table in the house, but rightfully so, the wealthiest woman in the room had it. She sat at the table, just as she would anytime she came to this club. Girls would surround the table because there were very important and wealthy men sitting with her.

Anytime she was there, the girls would stick out their butts and their tongues as they passed the table, trying to get the men's attention. The most entertaining thing about it was that they weren't always just trying to get the men's attention. Blac had become a very popular and sought-after woman. She was pretty powerful in the night world, and most women knew that she pretty much took care of the women around her, whether they worked with her or they were sleeping in her bed. Either way it went, if you were affiliated with her, you were good, and you had one of the more fantasy-like lives. While Blac had Charlie still, that never stopped anything that she had going on with the ladies, as long as they knew how to play their position.

A beautiful young woman came to the table where curly headed, sexy, well-dressed Blac was sitting and lighting a cigar and said, "Good evening, Blac. Is there anything else I can get for you?" with a sexy smirk.

Blac reached out her hand, placed it in the middle of the girl's back and said, "No, beautiful. That's everything for right now. If anything, I'll let you know."

The girl said, "OK, Blac, just let me know," and walked away from the table.

One of the men at the table turned and nearly broke his neck trying to look at the waitress as she walked away. Blac loudly cleared her throat. The man looked back at Blac and said, "Oh, my bad. I almost forgot where I was and who I was with."

Blac laughed and put her elbows on the table. She looked at him and said, "Clearly, you a little horny tonight, I see."

The man laughed and said, "Well, that's why we're here. We here to look and conquer, right?"

Blac said, "Yes, something like that, but unfortunately for you, I've already pinned that one to the headboard."

The man choked and coughed and said, "Really? What was wrong with her?"

Blac said, "Nothing, nothing at all. Sweet girl, one of the baddest ones I've had, but I don't like runners."

The man said, "Oh, snap, Blac. She was crawling up the wall."

Blac laughed and said, "Like a family of roaches in the projects."

The man looked at Blac and said, "Well, in that case, which one of these girls are you taking home tonight? 'Cause I know you taking somebody down." He slapped one of the girls who was walking by on the butt. The girl looked back at him and said, "Sir, don't put your hands on me."

Blac reached her hands out and said, "Baby girl, I'm sorry. He's an animal fresh out the cage and he don't know how to act." The woman said, "Blac, you right. I know a real dog when I see

120

one."

The man started barking and said, "Yes, big dog," as he grabbed the crotch part of his pants.

Blac looked at him and said, "Well, you know what dogs got."

The man said, "No," as he looked at the woman with his flirting eyes.

Blac looked at him and said, "Fleas!"

The woman laughed and walked away.

The man looked at Blac and said, "But I got my tetanus shot, so I'm good."

Blac shook her head, looked at another man who was sitting across from her and said, "Paul, you sure is quiet tonight."

Paul, the gentleman sitting across from Blac at the table and smoking a cigar, said, "I know how to be quiet when grown folks are speaking."

Blac said, "Oh, do you? 'Cause from what I'm hearing, you don't," as she ashed her cigar in a glass ashtray to her left.

Paul leaned into the table and said, "Lady, I don't follow what you trying to say, so say it with your chest." The atmosphere became tense as the eyes of the gentlemen at the table went back and forth as the two exchanged words.

Paul said, "You always got a lot to say. You are probably one of the most disobedient, big-mouthed women I ever met in my life. You don't know how to just play Charlie's nice little wife and leave the real affairs to the big men. You always wanna get in the middle of something. I guess that's why you always got so much trouble." Blac took a sip from her glass of champagne and said, "See, that's where you messed up. I'm not Charlie's little wife. He got one of those, and it ain't me. That's first. Second, what do you mean, 'let the big men handle their affairs'? Boy, I'm bigger than anybody in this room *and* at this table." She looked around at the men. No one objected to what she was saying, so it must be true.

She slammed her glass down, not breaking it, and said,

"Don't let this curly hair, six-inch heels and perfect body fool you. I'm nothing to play with, with or without Charlie. Paul, I'm only going to tell you one time and one time only: Stop running your mouth about my business, stop saying stuff about my girls and stop saying stuff about me. Because you know one thing about running faucets."

Paul looked at Blac, sucked his teeth and said, "No, I don't know about running faucets, but I'm pretty sure you gon' tell me." Blac looked Paul in the face and said, "You can bet'cho unborn child I'm about to tell you. Water faucets get cut off by the water company, and I don't like floods, so I clean mines up early."

Paul stepped away from the table and said, "Out of respect for the late Prince and Charlie, I'm going to go ahead and call it a night. Because no matter how big of a boss you are, you still wear skirts, so I'm not going to even entertain what you just said. But I'ma tell you one thing: I don't take kindly to threats."

Blac laughed and said, "You know my rep. I don't make threats; I make *promises.*"

The man, who seemed to be playful and flirtatious with the ladies up until now, seemed to change his demeanor. He now seemed to be nervous about what he was watching unfold. He looked at Paul and Blac and said, "It gotta be a better way to handle this. I'm gonna need everybody to calm down."

Blac looked at the man out of the corner of her right eye and said, "I'm calm. I haven't stood up, I haven't raised my voice. I'm very calm. I always stay calm."

The man looked back at Blac and said, "OK, that's good. Thank you." He looked up at Paul, who was standing over the table and had packed up as if he was about to leave. He said, "We've had a good day today. Settle down and just sit it out. You know Blac don't take no mess from nobody, not even us. Just chill out; she don't mean no harm."

Blac looked at him and said, "Don't speak for me."

He said, "BLAC!"

Blac picked up her phone and searched for the contact that read "Protégé." She texted Protégé a green heart, which symbolized that Paul had written a check that he couldn't cash and his life was now at the mercy of the nice lady who he had just stuck his chest out at. A loud *ding* played on Asia's phone as she sat at the bar, peeping out the scene and seeing who was at the club. She was very discreet and did not talk to very many people. People would walk up to her and speak to her because they knew who she was, but she kept all of her conversations to a duration of one minute or less. Asia was actually on a job, and anybody who knew her knew that when she was on a job, she was *very* focused and determined on whoever her target was. The message on her phone came from a contact called "Boss" and displayed a green heart. Asia read the message, put her phone back into her pocketbook, finished her glass of champagne and paid her bill. An older Black gentleman, who was her bartender, looked back and said, "You're leaving?"

Asia responded by smirking and saying, "No, I'm going to dance ."

The man nodded up and down and resumed cleaning a glass with a bar towel.

Asia walked to the dance floor and started dancing. She danced in a way that was so sexy that everybody in the club was staring at her. In a short period of time, Asia got the attention of Blac's table. Paul, who had calmed down by this time, looked over his shoulder to get a better view. At this time, Paul sat back down and joined Blac and the three other men who were sitting at the table. Another important person who seemed to be hypnotized was the lead saxophone player in the band, and his name was Jacob. Jacob was a very nice and loving young man. He came from a good family with a good upbringing, but his parents taught him to follow his dreams. So, he worked a day job and followed his dream by night, playing in the band that played at The Black Silhouette. The most interesting thing about Jacob was that he had no connections to the game—or, to better phrase it, the dark side—so he was not fully aware of who Asia was. All he knew was that Asia was a beautiful woman who was mysterious to him and would come and steal the dance floor with her beautiful body and radiant face. He had made several passes at Asia, but they all went unnoticed. Asia left the dance floor, walked up to the table where Blac and the four men sat and put her hands around Paul's shoulder, sliding them down the front of his chest. She said, "Hey, Paul. Wanna dance?"

Paul turned, looked at Asia and said, "With you? Absolutely. Wait, how did you know my name?"

Asia told Paul, "Everybody knows who you are, Paul."

Asia led Paul onto the dance floor and they very intensely danced together for the next several songs. This did not make Jacob upset, because while he was playing it cool, he would simply think about her dancing with him instead of the guy she was dancing with. This wasn't the first time that Jacob had played a background role while Asia danced with another guy. He was just happy that he could witness such a sight. Paul looked into Asia's eyes and said, "Miss Pretty, tell me something."

Asia swung her body and said, "I'll tell you anything."

Paul said, "Are you into fetishes?"

Asia leaned into his face and said, "What kind of fetishes?" Paul signaled her to come closer to him with his hands. Asia came closer to Paul and started dancing again. Paul whispered in her ear something that was entertaining and jaw-dropping to her. Asia smirked and continued dancing with him as the song ended. The lead singer in the band said, "We're going to take a couple of minutes to get ready for our next set. We'll be back in five." Asia looked at Paul and said, "Good. I need to use the little girl's room."

Paul and Asia parted ways as Asia walked to the bathroom and Paul walked back to the table. Paul was now at the table alone. Blac and the other guys moved throughout the club and they were no longer sitting. Paul scanned the room, looking for the guys. Each of them was having a conversation in a corner with a beautiful young lady. They figured that Paul was enjoying himself, so they should as well. He looked at his friends and they paid him no attention, but when he looked at Blac, she looked at him, smirked and blew him a kiss. Blac had no worries because she already knew his destiny, which she had so generously set up for him. With disgust, he turned his head, rolled his eyes and lifted a glass of champagne to his lips. There's a saying, "Don't mess with people who prepare your food or take care of your children because you never know what can happen to you as a result." While Paul was still angry with Blac, he seemed to forget that he had just left the very glass of champagne he was drinking at the table with her. Paul continued to sit at the table and enjoy his champagne, waiting for Asia to come out of the bathroom and getting ready for the next set of music. Asia walked out of the bathroom, closing her pocketbook and heading back to the dance floor. As she walked out of the ladies' room, she saw Jacob standing against the wall. Jacob stopped Asia and said, "Hey, pretty lady."

Asia looked at Jacob and said, "Hey, boy. Shouldn't you be getting ready for the next set?"

Jacob looked at Asia and said, "The name is Jacob."

Asia said, "OK. Well, Jacob, what's up?"

Jacob looked at Asia, leaned back against the wall and said, "Why is something so beautiful so mean?"

Asia looked at Jacob. She said, "Listen, I got to get back to the dance floor. So, unless you got something worth keeping me here, you might wanna let me go on with my night."

Jacob said, "I could change your life," as he grabbed his crotch.

Asia looked down at Jacob's hand, laughed and said, "Boy, you wouldn't know what to do with me if I gave it to you on a platter."

Jacob looked at Asia and said, "You wanna try me?"

Asia stepped closer to Jacob. She took her pointer finger and stroked it down the front of his shirt all the way down to his belt buckle. As her finger touched his belt buckle, she looked at him and said, "You *are* kind of cute. Green as the grass, but kinda cute. You might not have enough junk in your pants, though." As she gripped his belt buckle and unfastened it, Jacob began to get nervous. He looked down at Asia's hands, wondering what she was doing. Asia unfastened Jacob's belt buckle and unzipped his pants. She then spit in the palm of her right hand and stuck it into Jacob's pants until it disappeared and all they could see was the outline of an object moving around in his dress pants. Jacob's jaw dropped right away. She put her left hand on the wall behind Jacob's head and leaned in toward him aggressively. She grabbed his cock and whispered in his ear.

"Oh, yeah, you like that, don't you? You like when I stroke it, don't you?"

Jacob squinted his eyes tightly as his forehead and hands sweated like he was outside on a hot Georgia day.

Asia said, "Hmm, you like that, don't you? See, I know what you like. Mama knows what you like."

Jacob tried to move Asia's hand, but she pushed her body into his and started breathing heavily, matching Jacob's breaths.

"No, Papa. This is what you wanted and you got it. Now, what I need you to do for me…"

Jacob, while fighting the urge to enjoy this moment, closed his eyes tightly. Jacob shook his head no.

Asia said, "No?! Now, you know I don't know what that means." She licked the sweat off of Jacob's face and said, "Mmm, bacon. Maple bacon, at that."

She laughed and threw her head back as Jacob gasped for breath and fought the urge to moan.

Asia leaned in closer to Jacob and whispered in his ear, "Now, what I need you to do is make that big boy speak."

Asia gripped his wood tighter, stroking it harder and faster, and said, "Yes, speak." She put her face and lips as close to his face as she could without touching him and said, "Make that pole speak… spit… bam!"

Jacob squeezed his butt cheeks together, lifted his heels off of the ground and, in a deep voice, said "Ahhh." He gasped and breathed very heavily as a thick, creamy, white-gray secretion of semen oozed out of his body, onto Asia's hands and all over his clothes. Asia let go of his cock and very sexily walked into the ladies' room. Jacob's body fell against the wall and he exhaled with his pants still open. Exposed, he said, "Wow," as he took in what

126

Asia had just done to him. He looked down at his pants and realized that the secretion had gotten all over them, so he panicked and ran out of the club, knocking over people as he ran, and disappeared for the rest of the night.

Asia washed her hands and returned to the dance floor, where the band had started their next set—but, of course, without their lead saxophone player. It's a good thing they had a backup. Asia found Paul at the table; she took him by the hand and led him to the dance floor. They danced to a couple more songs; as they danced, they laughed and Paul whispered very erotic things in Asia's ear. Paul was a different type of man that represented an different type of sexual lifestyle. He had a different type of excitement. Paul found excitement in pain more so than pleasure—actually, pain *was* his pleasure. He whispered all types of fetishes and scenarios in Asia's ear. While this was not the first time she had heard these things in her line of work, she was surprised that this extremely influential businessman was involved in such activities, but there was nothing wrong with that because we all have our kinks—even you. She agreed with him and said whatever she needed to in order to get him where she needed to so that she could do what she needed to do to him. She was all in. Paul was one of few men that recognized that the man body have different g spots and he had and was willing to explore all of them.

Asia stopped and said, "Give me a minute. I gotta go by the bar."

Paul agreed to the heads-up and allowed Asia to walk away from him. She walked to the bar, asked the bartender for a piece of paper and a pen and wrote down an address. She folded the piece of paper, put it in Paul's palm and said, "Give me an hour and come to this address." She closed his hand very tightly around the paper as she walked out of the club. As she left, the heads of all the men and women in the club turned to watch her. In a corner across the room was Blac cutting her eyes, watching everything that had just unfolded between Asia and Paul. Then Blac, too, faded into the night.

About an hour later, Paul showed up at a hotel where he was greeted by sexy lingerie-, heel- and makeup-wearing Asia. Asia opened the room door holding a glass of champagne. When he entered the room, he could see that there was a champagne bottle chilling on a bucket of ice on the table. There was also another glass, and it was empty. Now, Paul arrived at the room pretty dysfunctional and messed up from all the liquor and champagne he had consumed at The Black Silhouette. Asia knew this, and it helped with what she was trying to do as far as luring him to the room. Asia sat on the bed and looked at Paul; he looked like he had way too much to drink. Paul was fighting to keep balance of his head while sitting in the chair.

Asia asked Paul, "Would you like a glass of champagne?" Sluggish Paul shook his head no as he could barely stand to keep his eyes open. Paul wasn't just drunk. It seemed like somebody had drugged him. The drugs were actually starting to weigh down on his spirit but didn't completely take over because he was a partier. Paul's head was spinning, and he fought to keep his eyes open.

Asia looked at Paul and said, "Come on, now. Don't make me drink alone. There's a whole bottle! Don't make me drink alone; you can have just one," in a very sure and sultry voice.

Paul was able to pull himself together and said, "You know what? I *will* have one glass, because I wouldn't have thought in a million years that I would be in this room with you. You're so beautiful and I've heard such good things about you."

Asia looked at Paul and said, "Have you?"

Paul said, "Yes, I've heard *very* good things about you."

Asia looked at Paul and said, "Well, let's just hope that those things are all true and that you can be someone that speaks very highly of me as well."

Paul looked at Asia and said, "I don't doubt that for a second. I'm pretty sure that I won't be able to forget you after tonight."

Asia looked at Paul and said, "You have no idea."

Asia and Paul sat together and both put down a glass of champagne as Asia put on very erotic and techno-like music. In normal cases, Asia would have played slow music that had a suspenseful type of beat to it, but based on what she was doing and the type of man Paul was, she wanted to put techno music on. Everything had to stay upbeat in order for what she was doing to actually work. As Asia ripped off Paul's clothes, he tilted his head back. Asia started feeling and kissing all over his chest. She stroked her tongue from one side of his chest to the other, gently kissing and sucking on his nipples as Paul gasped in enjoyment. Asia got off of Paul, stood on her feet, walked to the bed and started feeling under it. Asia pulled out what looked like a carryout container from under the bed. She threw it on the top of the bed and opened it, revealing a zipper down the middle of it. When she opened it, Paul popped his head to the right and back to the front in order to see what she was pulling out. She was pulling out any submissive man's *dream* toolkit—in it were whips, chains, mouth gags, anal plugs, paddles, feathers and long wooden rods, just to name a few things. Paul looked at Asia as he stroked his tongue from one side of his mouth to the other, shaking his head up and down.

"I knew I liked you for a reason. We're gonna have a lot of fun with these," he said, breathing heavily.

Asia opened the refrigerator and took out a bag that contained an apple, a cucumber and a long carrot. Asia said, "Oh, we are about to have *more* fun than you've *ever* had in your life."

Paul got a boost of energy from the exciting anticipation of what was to come. Allowing him to spring out the chair aggressively grabbing and kissing Asia as he walked her to the wall, he slammed Asia into the corner, holding both of her hands over her head and kissing her neck. Paul quickly spun Asia around and put her nose in the connecting point of the two walls. Paul took her hair and stroked his hands through it until he got to the middle of her head. He gripped a patch of her hair and yanked her head back as he sucked on her neck. Asia closed her eyes and held very still as this crazy man basically ate her up. Asia quickly snapped out of whatever trance the music and Paul had put her in. She untangled Paul's claws from her hair and yanked away from him, then pushed him onto the chair.

She ripped his cloth pants open as she took a feather and a wooden rod off of the bed, tracing it around his groin area. Paul threw his head back yet again and closed his eyes as Asia tickled his human meat. He went to grab his shaft. As his hand gripped his meat, Asia smacked his hand with the wooden rod. Paul quickly removed his hand.

Asia said, "Now, what do you think you are doing? That thang belongs to me and I didn't say you could touch it."

Paul sat back in the chair with head back as his boner stood up like a third leg sitting on his lap. Asia stopped touching him and walked over to the table where they had sat both their glasses of champagne; Asia picked up her glass and took a sip. Asia looked at Paul; by the look on his face, he appeared to still be enjoying himself. Asia smirked as she walked over to him. She dropped her body down in front of Paul, put her tongue on the roof of her mouth, pulled up a thick piece of saliva from her throat and covered Paul's shaft with it. She then aggressively gripped his meat while shoving it down her throat hard and fast. Paul, under Asia's direction, stroked the back of Asia's throat with his enormous erection. This became a mental game in which Asia would see how much of this king cobra she could slide down her throat without choking. Asia continued to massage Paul's mandingo with the muscles and saliva in her throat. When Asia peeked out of her left eye, she realized that Paul was enjoying himself too much. She quickly stood up and Paul dropped his hands to his sides, dangling them, almost touching the ground as if Asia had just sucked the soul out of him. Asia looked at Paul and smacked his meat hard with her hand.

"Ahhh!" screamed Paul.

Asia jumped and said, "Oh, that hurt, hun?"

Turned on, Paul sat up in the chair with his pants to his ankles and said, "Yeah, baby, do it again. Abuse him. He's been a bad boy; abuse him," biting his bottom lip.

Asia grabbed Paul by the back of his head and said, "Oh, yeah, you a freak."

Asia swiped everything on the bed to the floor, walked Paul

to the bed and threw him onto his stomach. Asia took a silk strap and tied his legs together, leaving his bottoms at his ankles. Then, Asia put a black silk blindfold over Paul's eyes. Paul licked his lips with excitement as Asia tied his arms to the headboard. Nicole opened the door, walked in the room and started gathering all of Asia's things. Nicole handed Asia a pair of black gloves and stood by the door with the bags.

Paul lifted up his head and said, "Hey, what you doing?" Asia said, "Don't worry. I'm here, Pa," while rolling her eyes. She reached out to Nicole. Nicole looked confused, then smirked, reached in her pocket and pulled out a long, slender metal vibrator. Asia wiped it off, then turned it on and stuck it in Paul's ass. Paul yelled out, "geeesssh That's what I'm talking about," and began grunting and moaning. Asia looked at Nicole and both of them smirked. Asia got her coat out of the closet and grabbed a nine inch carrot from the table. Asia looked at Paul and said, "Oh, Paul, you like that, don't you?"

Paul said, "Yes, baby! I love it! *Love* it! Gimme more! Gimme more!"

Asia put her foot on Paul's spine and said, "Well, you're gonna worship me after this."

Paul said, "Oh yeah, baby. Make me worship you."

Asia pulled the metal vibrator out of Paul and shoved the carrot so far up his anus that she thought she was touching his large intestine. Asia stuck that carrot so far up Paul's ass that all she could see was its stem. And the killer part is, she ain't even lube it up—just raw-dogged him.

Paul yelled, "Damn, baby... ah... I'm coming!"

Asia said, "Come on, Pa. Come."

Paul's body shook and his head slammed on the bed.

Asia said, "You done, Pa?"

Paul exhaled and said, "Yes, beautiful. That was amazing."

Asia said, "No, *Blac* is amazing."

Confused, Paul lifted his head and said, "Blac?"

Asia said, "Yes, you big-mouthed, musty bastard! Blac!" and

then shot Paul in the back of his head twice. Asia walked over to the door, opened it, grabbed a bag from Nicole, left the room and closed the door.

The next day, Asia and Blac met up for lunch. They decided to sit outside at a restaurant because it was a beautiful day. The restaurant had white tables and white chairs; its balcony had brass railings that were covered by big plants and leaves. The ground had palm trees sprouting out of it, the scene was a beautiful, classic *Miami Vice* type of vibe and the waiters and waitresses walked throughout the interior and exterior of the restaurant serving the guests in all white clothing, with button-down shirts and black shoes. Around their waists were white aprons in which they would hold their receipt books, pens and notepads.

"Here you are, ma'am," said Blac.

Asia looked at the stack of money that Blac had handed her inside of a yellow envelope.

"Is it all there?" asked Asia.

Blac chuckled and said, "It better be all there. I counted it myself."

Asia said, "Nah, I'm just playing. I believe you. I know you wouldn't trick me or cheat me."

Blac said, "If I ain't got nothing else, I got some money, so I definitely don't need to trick you."

Asia looked at Blac and said, "At least that problem is taken care of and you don't have to worry about it anymore."

Blac leaned back in her chair and said, "Yeah, you right about that. But have you thought anymore about what I said to you when we were in the office?"

Asia said, "What exactly are you talking about?"

Blac said, "You finding a hobby or figuring out something else to do with your time other than this."

Asia said, "I don't have much time for anything else. Plus, that's not where my focus is. My focus is just stacking my money and just letting this be what it is, letting it take its course, and when it's the end, it's the end."

Blac said, "That's cute... and *stupid*. Don't give me any 'live on the edge,' 'pursuit of happiness' and 'not planning for the worst' quotes. Don't be ignorant and not have an escape plan. I don't like the way that sounds for you. I feel like you have so much more potential and you could do so much more. It was cool at the beginning because you didn't know better, but we've been doing this for a while now, so by this time, you should know what you wanna do next and you should have a plan to work towards. Failure to plan is preparation to fail. Don't get so caught up in this life that you have nothing to fall back on because you've let all your other talents go to waste or pass you by to the point where your passion is gone and all you wanna do is hoe.

Asia looked at Blac and said, "Blac, we are who we are."

Blac said, No, Asia. You are who *I* created you to be and who *I* wanted you to be, so just remember it's a life outside of this and keep that in mind when you're out here moving around and doing things. I don't ever wanna put you in no position where I can't protect you, and I sure as hell don't want you to put me in a position where I can't protect myself.

Asia said, "I can understand that."

Blac turned her head, looked around and said, "Where is this waiter at? I'm thirsty."

Asia put her head into the menu and said, "I don't know. I guess they should be here in a couple minutes."

A fine, familiar-faced young man quickly walked through the aisle to their table with a notepad in his hand. The man started apologizing, saying, "Hey, ladies. Sorry about the wait. What can I get for you?"

Blac's eyes got big as she looked at the gentleman. She crossed her arms over her chest and said, "Um... look up, Asia." Asia looked at the waiter, started smiling and shook her head. Blac said, "Boy you is a *brave* soul to show your face around this city after what you did last night! Or, should I say, what *she* did to you last night!"

The gentleman looked at Blac and said, "Ma'am, I'm not

sure I know what you're talking about."

Blac waved her hand from left to right and said, "No, no, no. Don't play no formal games with me, Jacob. I know exactly who you are. And you better hope you still got a job with the band, considering you ran out on them last night. But I understand why... you kind of had a mess," and burst out laughing. Jacob looked at both ladies, then looked around the restaurant to make sure that no one else had heard them or knew what they were talking about. He tried to hush Blac so that she wouldn't embarrass him or draw too much attention to what she was saying, but if you knew anything about Blac, you knew you couldn't shut her up. She was gonna say whatever she was saying, no matter how you felt about what she was saying.

Blac waved her hand at Jacob and said, "Boy, don't nobody care about your little situation. Next time, just walk around with Kleenex or something wet in your pockets and then you won't have to go all the way home. But I'm glad you did go home, 'cause don't nobody wanna be smelling that the whole time you perform. And like I said, you better hope you still got a job."

Jacob turned to Asia and said, "Well, hello, Asia."

Asia put her right hand behind her ear removing her hair from her face and said, "Hello, Jacob. How are you doing today?"

Jacob said, "I'm just fine, considering what you did to me last night."

Asia looked at Jacob and said, "Well, that's what happens when you're a little boy who wanna play grown man games. I'm a grown woman and I've been that way for a long time. I don't play no games, so when you come at me, you better be ready for whatever you trying to do. 'Cause if not, I'ma school you every time.

Blac looked at Asia and said, "I know that's right. Well, clearly, I've gotten in my seven chuckles for the day and I got some other things I need to tend to, so I will leave you two to it. I'll be in touch, Asia. Don't get lost."

Asia looked at Blac and said, "What do you mean? I'd never get lost. And I thought we were having lunch." Blac grabbed her big black purse and said, "Oh, no, love! I have seemed to have lost my appetite, so I'll run." She stood face-to-face with Jacob and looked him up and down before walking out of the restaurant.

Jacob sat down at the table and said, "Tell me something. What do you do?"

Asia said, "Why?"

Jacob said, "Because I wanna know what type of business you're into. Y'all got these really nice clothes, your hair's always really nice, you have all these diamonds and you get to drive all these nice cars. Whatever y'all do, you must do well at it, because you have really nice things."

Asia said, "We do what we do."

Jacob said, "Don't go stiff for me."

Asia started laughing and said, "No, I'll leave that up to you." Jacob sarcastically laughed and said, "Yeah, you're so funny. But no, for real, what do you do?"

Asia looked at him in his face as she put both of her arms on the table. She crossed them on top of each other and said, "You really wanna know what I do?"

Jacob said, "Yes that's why I asked."

Asia said, "All those people with those nice cars and that nice jewelry and stuff you like? They like to have sex. And they don't like to have sex with just anybody, so they pick the best females that's most suitable to what they're looking for. They pay them really good money to spend a night, sometimes two, sometimes a weekend, even a week with them. These women live very comfortable lives. Any other questions?"

Jacob said, "Let me guess, you're one of those women. Well, I know you're busy, so let me get this straight: You stay with these men, and when you sleep with one, they give you whatever you want?"

Asia said, "Basically. You got a problem with that?"

Jacob made a face and said, "No, I don't. At least you got some type of standard about yourself. You're not just letting your emotions control your life. At least you have some type of substance and focus and standard to what you're doing." Asia turned up her lip because she felt like he was not being genuine and just saying whatever she wanted to hear in order to have a conversation with her.

Asia said, "Sure, Jacob. Standards are standards."

Jacob looked at Asia and said, "Hey, why don't you let me take you out on a date?"

Asia grabbed her envelope off of the table, stuck it in her purse and said, "I don't think so."

Jacob said, "Why not? I'm a nice guy and I could show you a good time without sex."

Asia looked at him and said, "Is that so?"

Jacob said, "Yeah. I mean, I don't have as much money as you probably do, and I probably won't be able to show you nothing crazy expensive, but I can show you something really nice that'll really interest you. And I don't care about you being an escort. You do what you gotta do to get your money. That's your business! I just wanna show you a good time and hopefully get to know you." Asia said, "I don't know what it is that you want or why you don't get it, but I'm not interested."

Jacob said, "Why you gotta be so mean? I'm just trying to show you a good time and show you a life outside of what you do where you could let your hair down a little bit and just enjoy it and not worry about somebody trying to get in your pants at the end of the night."

Asia's mind started wandering and she couldn't help but wonder, *Was this guy sent by a higher power to defer me from the lifestyle I'm living?* Asia quickly snapped out of it, looked at Jacob and said, "You still gon' try to get in my pants."

Jacob said, "What man wouldn't? But at least if I take you on a date, you don't have to feel obligated to do anything, and if you do, it's your choice. So, what do you say?"

Asia put her head to the sky and said, "You cute. I guess I can spend an afternoon with you. I'll go on a date with you, but under one circumstance."

136

Jacob grinned from ear to ear like he just experienced his first boner and said, "I'm listening."

Asia said, "I get to pick the location *and* I get to pick the type of date."

Jacob looked at Asia and said, OK, that's cool. So, can I have your number so I can text you?"

Asia said, "I guess you could. Don't be a stalker, 'cause I *will* block you if you do."

Jacob said, "Oh, I understand. I'm pretty sure you will, so I won't do anything stupid. I'll be the perfect gentleman."

Asia looked at him and said, "Yeah, right. Well, let me get everything settled and together, and I will hit you up this afternoon. Then, we can go from there."

Jacob said, "OK. Sounds like a plan."

The next day, Jacob entered the dock of a big beautiful yacht. This yacht was at Lake Erie that was accessible from Ontario Canada to the north and the US states such as Michigan, Ohio, Pennsylvania and most of all New York to all four directions. Jacob had never experienced anything like this. A man outside of the yacht signaled Jacob to come on, so he did. When he came down the stairs, an older Black gentleman greeted him, "Hello, Jacob. Miss Asia awaits your arrival."

Out of one of the corners of the interior part of the boat and headed towards Jacob was a fuchsia sundress-wearing, curly-headed Asia. Asia had her makeup done flawlessly and held two glasses and a bottle of champagne in her hands.

"Hello, Jacob," said Asia. "How are you doing, sir?"

Jacob shook his head up and down and said, "Not too shabby. And speaking of not being too shabby, this yacht is not too shabby! You own this?"

Asia shook her head, rolled her eyes and said, "No, Jacob, I don't own it. It's a rental. But it's beautiful, isn't it, Jacob?"

Jacob said, "It's probably one of the most beautiful things I've ever seen in my life."

Asia said, "More beautiful than me?"

Jacob said, "Of course not," and they both laughed. Asia sat down and Jacob joined her. Asia removed the foil like paper from the champagne bottle and proceeded to pop the cork and pour two glasses. Asia said, "Well, drink up! There's more where that came from."

Jacob said, "Well, let's make a toast."

Asia said, "OK. What are we toasting to?"

Jacob said, "We are toasting to new life and to you being nice to me this whole day."

Asia laughed and said, "OK, I can toast to that."

Both of them toasted and took a sip from their glasses. In front of them was a small table. The older gentleman standing over Asia said, "Miss Asia, is there anything else I can do for you right now?"

Asia said, "No, George. I'm fine right now, but we will let you know if we need anything."

The man said, "Yes, ma'am. I'll be right over here."

Asia said, "OK, thank you, George." The older gentleman walked away towards the front of the yacht and went upstairs to the outdoor part of the yacht; he left to give Asia and Jacob some privacy. Asia sat back on the luxury sofa in the room and said, "So, tell me, Jacob, what is your family like?"

Jacob sat back and said, "Well, my family are pretty plain Jane, working people. Not too much excitement. My mother was a nurse and my father was a garbage man."

Asia sat up and said, "Ew."

Jacob laughed and said, "Yeah, I know. But believe it or not, he never stunk!"

Asia looked at him and said, "I don't believe that! A garbage man who don't stink? Yeah, OK."

Jacob said, "No, really! My dad never stunk. I've never heard my mom complain about him and I never smelled any stench myself. He probably was one of the cleanest people I've ever known, male *or* female.

Asia said, "Wow, that's crazy! So, your mom was a nurse?

That's interesting."

Jacob looked at her and said, "Oh, yeah? How so?"

Asia said, "Believe it or not, I started out as a nurse."

Jacob said, "I believe it. You look like a smart one."

Asia said, "What does that mean?"

Jacob lifted his hands up and said, "Hold on! Don't shoot! All I'm saying is that you look like somebody who has a background. You look like you have other things that you could be doing besides what you're doing. Not to say that what you're doing is bad or there's anything wrong with it. I just feel like there's more to you than that."

Asia said, "Relax. I'm not gonna choke you for being honest. I get what you're saying."

Jacob sat back and said, "Good, because I don't have time to be fighting with you on this date. I'm trying to be as good as possible and make this date go as smooth as it can."

Asia said, "It will, long as you know how to talk."

Jacob said, "I'm trying."

Asia said, "Well, you're not doing too bad right now. But yeah, back to what I was saying: I went to school to be a nurse, but I decided I didn't wanna do it because I didn't wanna work for anybody. I wanted to do something where I basically worked for myself and I did my own thing."

Jacob looked at her and said, "But... don't you work for Blac?"

Asia rolled her eyes and said, "Now you just ruined it." Jacob said, "No, I didn't mean to ruin it! I'm sorry. I didn't mean that. Forget I said that."

Asia said, "No, you clearly don't know what you're talking about, so let me school you. I don't work for Blac; I work *with* Blac. I'm just as much of an asset to her life as she is to mines. Oh, and we don't do the same thing, so you don't have to worry about it." Jacob said, "Yeah, 'cause I heard Blac ain't nothing to play with."

Asia said, "She ain't, but that's besides the point. We not here to talk about Blac, 'cause one thing for certain, two things for sure: I don't talk about other people business when they ain't here to defend themselves."

Jacob said, "That's fair. Well, tell me about your family."

Asia said, "It's not much to tell. My father was a banker. Oh, and my mother was an entrepreneur."

Jacob said, "Well, at least we know where you get it from." Asia laughed and said, "Yeah, I got a lot of my mother in me. She was wonderful, probably the most iconic woman I knew, and my dad was so structured. I think that's why I'm so structured with the way I do things and why discipline and being responsible for your actions are important to me."

He said, "Yo' daddy wasn't a thug and yo' mama wasn't a hoe?"

Asia rolled her eyes again and said, "You have to stop watching so much TV and movies. Not everybody who gets into this business is from a horrible background and not everybody's parents made them get into it. So, no, I don't have a hoe background or a street background. I basically seen the opportunity for me to be my own boss and do something that I pretty much knew about. Plus, I like to have sex, so it works for me."

Jacob said, "That was TMI. I'm trying to be good, so "I'ma need you to be a little bit more PG-13. Matter of fact, just be PG when you talking to me about your life."

Asia looked at Jacob and said, "Well, don't ask questions you don't really want the answer to."

Jacob said, "No. I want all the answers."

Asia said, "Well, shut up and listen. Like I was saying before I was rudely interrupted, my dad was a banker and my mother was an entrepreneur. She actually sold sexy lingerie out of our home and she did pretty well with it."

Jacob said, "OK, that sounds cool. So, how did you get into the life?"

Asia said, "I met somebody who knew some people who knew some other people. I met with the people and that's basically how it happened."

Jacob said, "That's such a vague explanation, but I get it."

140

Asia said, "I figured you would."

Jacob looked at Asia and said, "Well, look. I ain't got all the money and excitement you're used to, but I definitely can be a good companion and support system to you. What you do is what you do and I ain't never been the type of man to stress or belittle a woman because of her hustle. At least you got one, and from what I can see, you do well for yourself. What kind of man would I be to interfere with that? Oh, and I ain't worried about what you do with your body, long as you being safe and discreet. I like you, and the more I talk to you, the more intrigued I become. I ain't worried but no tricks, especially since I know they can't make ya toes curl like I'ma do." Asia stroked her hand across her thighs and said, "You're pretty confident, aren't you?"

Jacob said, "Come on, Mama. I'm a musician. We make love and drive 'em crazy.

Asia said, "I bet," as her mind wandered. She already knew that he was worth her time, and she knew his size; she was just interested to know how it felt. Asia sucked her teeth and said, "Boy, stop capping. I touched you for two minutes and you exploded." Jacob said, "I was not about to walk around with cement balls to prove a point. You got that. Plus, I ain't know you was a gangsta."

Asia looked at Jacob and said, "Are you hungry?"

Jacob looked at Asia and said, "Why? You got some food?" Asia and Jacob stood up and opened a door to another area of the yacht, where there were four-course meal options. Jacob was able to taste different foods prepared by a private chef. The best part about the location is that they were able to enjoy some of the best dishes in the country and they did.

Jacob looked at Asia and said, "Yeah, your date is a lot better than mine would have been."

Asia and Jacob conversed, laughed, talked and enjoyed each other's company while tasting the different foods. They enjoyed themselves so much that time had gotten away from them and they ended up staying on the yacht until the evening time. When they got ready to leave each other, it was dark outside. They exited the yacht together, hand in hand. Jacob helped Asia down and jumped onto the dock.

Jacob looked at Asia and said, "I really had a good time with you."

Asia said, "Surprisingly, I enjoyed your company as well."

Jacob said, "Well, where do we go from here?"

Asia said, "Well, I haven't had my daily nap, so I'm gonna say goodnight. Maybe I'll call you tomorrow."

Jacob said, "I would really like that."

Asia said, "I guess I can do that for you."

Jacob said, "Well, let me walk you to your car.

Asia said, "No, I got it. You're fine."

Jacob said, "OK, that's cool. Well, you enjoy your night, beautiful, and I hope to talk to you soon," and they parted ways.

CHAPTER 11
INTIMACY /LIMIT

"Daddy need smoke. The coop need a pair of shoes?" a young Black man sang to himself as he pushed a cart full of linens and cleaning supplies. This young man was the housekeeper on duty at the hotel. He walked into one of the rooms and stopped singing as his jaw dropped. He was stunned at what he saw.

The young man said, "What happened in here? His wife must've left him and he couldn't take life no more. He got an empty glass of champagne, but where the bottle at? I need a drink... nah, he ain't do that to hisself, man! This is messed up and I ain't got time for this. I'm just trying to come, do my little shift and go home, got damn! It *would* be a dead man on my shift! I swear to God, I'm quitting today! I swear to God, I don't care what they got going on. I don't care who needs money, I don't care about being homeless, I'm quitting this job *today*! The young man picked up a walkie-talkie and a voice said, "Yes, sir?"

The young man said, "I quit."

The voice said, "I don't have time to play with you today. You always wanna play."

The young man stood in the room and said, "I'm not playing. It's a dead man in this room with something shoved up his ass and I'm not doing this. You don't pay me enough."

"The voice said, "Stop playing. That's not funny."

The young man said, "Nah, it's really a grown man in this room with something shoved up his ass and he dead. It look like he got two shots to the head. I don't know. He stinks. I'm not cleaning this room and I'm not doing nothing with moving this body. Matter of fact, I'm not even touching nothing. Matter of fact, forget what I just said. I wasn't even in this room."

The voice on the other side of the walkie-talkie panicked and said, "Let me call the police. Get out of that room."

The young man said, "Well, you ain't gotta tell me twice," walked out the room and closed the door.

A detective held a camera and snapped pictures of Paul's body. A pretty young woman walked through the room with an older man and greeted the detective.

"Hi, Lola. Welcome to paradise," the detective said.

Lola laughed and said, "It can't be that bad."

The detective said, "Oh, you have no idea what you're about to see. You ready?"

The three detectives stood over the bed. One of them pulled back what looked like a sheet to uncover Paul's dead body, which had been decaying.

Lola looked at the man and said, "Ew, he stinks really bad. How long has he been here?"

The detective looked at Lola and said, "You wanna laugh?"

Lola said, "No."

The detective said, "You wanna cry?"

Lola, annoyed, said, "No."

The detective said, "Well, get ready. He's been in this room for about three days."

Lola said, "What?! Who needs to get fired first?"

The detective said, "I'll let you handle that part of this. This is your current case, not mine."

Lola rolled her eyes and said, "Figures. Who is this man?"

The detective said, "The news just gets better and better. It's Paul."

Lola looked at him with a shocked face and said, "Paul Dunbar?"

The detective said, "Yes, Paul Dunbar. The famous and popular Paul Dunbar."

Lola said, "Who did he piss off?" while looking at his cold, dead body.

The detective said, "Based on his rap sheet, there's no telling."

Lola sighed and said, "Oh, my God! This man stinks so bad!"

She walked around the bed examining Paul's body as she noticed something very interesting. Lola looked at the detective and said, "Wait, why is he... I don't even wanna know. This looks like a sex game gone bad."

The detective shook his head up and down and said, "I was thinking the same thing, but I like to mind my business. Grown men do what grown men do."

Lola said, "Well, I'm not minding my business when a grown man ends up on my desk because he's no longer here."

The detective said, "Your point is fair. But this is your case, not mine, thank God."

Lola looked at Paul's body, noticing the carrot emerging from his anus, and said, "Is that...? Oh, no. Say this isn't so."

Lola's partner looked at her and laughed.

Lola said, "This is not funny! I don't want this case. I don't want anything to do with this case!"

The detective said, "Well, it sure *is* yours, and I'm pretty sure you're gonna figure it out fast."

Lola said, "Sure I am." Looking at the carrot, she grabbed one of the people dusting the room for forensic evidence and said, "Hey is it possible that we could find out what this is?"

The man replied, "I don't need to do an exam or even touch it to figure out what that is. That's a carrot. Like, the vegetable."

Lola looked back at her partner with a shocked face and said, "A carrot?! *Please* tell me I'm in the middle of a dream. This isn't real!"

Lola partner walked up beside her and said, "Well, we know that Paul Dunbar, the popular businessman, obviously brought someone to this room to have sex with him. At some point during the encounter, he got a carrot stuck inside of him and two shots to his head." Lola stood there, receiving what her partner had just said, and shook her head. Then, she said, "I can only think of one person who's brave enough to do this."

Lola's partner looked at her with a confused face and said, "Who are you thinking?"

Lola looked at her partner with a serious face and said, "Blac." Lola sucked her teeth, then turned and thanked the detective who had debriefed her, telling him that she would take the case from there. The detective wished her good luck as they all exited the room. Lola went to the front desk to speak to the head of reservations and housekeeping. They needed to be questioned for her investigation. Both of these positions were held by women, who were nervous in their uniforms as Lola and partner greeted them.

Lola said, "Hi, my name is Lola. I'm the head detective on this case, and this is John, my partner. I have a couple of questions. The first one is, why did it take so long for anybody to find this man? Don't you guys clean the rooms at checkout time every day?"

One of the young ladies, the reservation manager, said, "Normally, we do, but there was a note on the reservation for that specific room that stated not to go in there and clean it for three days because the guest was a high-profile person. We assumed that he didn't want anyone to go in the room because he had valuable things in there."

Lola said, "I see. Do you know who made the note on the reservation?"

The other woman raised her hand and said, "I made the note. Mr. Dunbar called on the evening that he came, before he arrived, and told us that he was coming. We didn't think anything of it because Mr. Dunbar usually comes here all the time. There was nothing suspicious about it."

Lola said, "Well, does Mr. Dunbar usually make those types of requests?"

The reservation manager said, "No; normally, he doesn't. But I didn't think that it was anything suspicious because of his status."

Lola said, "I understand that. So, when Mr. Dunbar came, did you check him in?"

The young lady said, "No. By that time, I was gone for the day. When Mr. Dunbar came to the hotel, he did not check in at the desk; he walked straight through as if he already knew his room number. But when I looked at the cameras, from what I can tell, when he came up to the room, that was the first time he came in for the night."

Lola said, "So, you didn't find anything about that to be suspicious?"

The young lady said, "No, because I just assumed that his security guard or someone else checked in for him."

Lola said, "Well, did they?"

The young lady said, "After finding his body and reviewing the camera footage, we saw no one who stuck out to us, but it was so busy that evening that anybody who had his information could have checked in for him."

Lola said, "Even a lady?"

The young lady said, "I doubt a lady could check in for him, since he's a man. The person checking in for him would have to be another man."

John said "we are going to need the surveillance footage for his floor"

Lola said, "Well, thank you, ladies. Here's my card. if you remember anything suspicious regarding Mr. Dunbar or that evening, please feel free to give me a call." Each of the ladies took a business card from Lola and returned to their work.

Lola looked at John and said, "So, whoever he was in the room with knew that they would need to check in for him without making themselves look suspicious. We're looking for either a man who checked in as Paul and committed the crime, or a woman who committed the crime and had a man check in for her to secure Paul's room."

John agreed and said, "Right. Well, we've got our work cut out for us."

Lola said, "Yeah. The pair pondered their thoughts for a second.

Then, Lola said, "Well, I think I've had enough excitement for today. My mind is going crazy and I'm completely drained from that sight, so I'm gonna call it a day. I'll meet you at the office first thing in the morning, at around 12."

John laughed and said, "Lola, that's pretty late in the morning."

Lola laughed and said, "Yeah, I know. I might have a long night, so it might take me a while to get in tomorrow."

John said, "OK. You gon' get in trouble!"

Lola looked at John and said, "After this case he just gave me, he better not even look at me wrong or else I'm transferring to another unit." John walked away from Lola and they both went about their days.

Lola got in her car and began to head home. She reflected on what she knew about the case and began to have flashbacks about her father. Lola's father's death was a traumatic experience for her, and in her adult life, she had a hard time dealing with it. Lola and her father was very close, so she got to see him during his highs and lows; she knew his strengths and weaknesses. Lola saw her dad as a loving and warm father who seemed to have two other sides that she wasn't too crazy about. Lola's dad was a flirtatious doctor who saw plenty of female patients; these patients would give him flirty looks and request that he come do home visits for them. Her father also experienced dark streaks from time to time, during which he would gamble and put the family's finances in jeopardy. This type of knowledge haunted Lola throughout her life and made her question the motivation for his death and the events surrounding it. She just couldn't understand how a loving father and husband could be executed like he was, and how no one had any answers about the killer. He was not only a loving father and husband; he also was the top award-winning doctor in the city and was loved by most people who knew him.

Just like me and you, he wasn't perfect—no one is. But his many perceptions and personas put him at risk, which ultimately led to his death; at least, that's what the story was. This raised so many questions for Lola and caused a strain on her and her mother's relationship. While her mother wanted to move on and not look too deep into the case, Lola couldn't help but wonder and have questions. These unanswered questions traumatized Lola and drove her to decide at a young age that she wanted to investigate and find the answers to unsolved mysteries such as her father's death. Based on her father's life, Lola felt that her killer could have been anybody: a female patient, a patient's husband, a man he gambled with, an obsessed client. There just was no telling. While on the police force, prior to becoming a detective, she would answer 187 calls—187 was the police code for murder.

During her time working as an officer on the street, Blac's name was frequently mentioned by veteran detectives, which made Blac a target in Lola's mind. While there was nothing that would directly connect Blac to any murders, due to the reputation of the people she was associated with and the nature of the crimes, she was always a conversation amongst most investigations. Lola had a strong vendetta against Blac for this reason. She never understood why this terrible person was able to walk the streets, and when she became a detective, she made it her business to work homicide cases in hopes of getting a break against Blac.

Lola walked into her home as her white teacup poodle ran up to her, barking and making noises. She closed the door with her jacket and briefcase in her hand. She was very tired and drained, feeling confused by the day that she had. There was a woman in the kitchen wearing grey sweatpants and a white T-shirt, with her curly blonde hair pulled up into a messy bun.

The woman said, "Hello, my love."

Lola walked up to the woman and kissed her on the lips. The woman looked at Lola and said, "What's wrong? You look stressed."

Lola said, "I am. Today was a long day."

As Lola walked into the living room to head towards the couch, the woman walked behind her and said, "Mi amor, would you like something to drink?"

Lola said, "Well, say less! A double shot of cognac, please." The woman said, "Yes, ma'am." She turned away and walked towards a glass cabinet. She reached into the cabinet and grabbed a short crystal glass. She walked to the kitchen and got two cubes of ice from the ice chest, put them in the glass, walked back to the glass cabinet and she sat the glass on top of the cabinet. She poured Lola a double shot of Hennessy. This was a fairly light-skinned woman who had freckles on her face, with full lips and tongue piercing. The woman walked in the living room with the glass in her hand. At this point, Lola had sat down with her poodle and turned on the TV. Lola took the glass from the woman and sat up completely, making room for her to sit down.

"Thanks, babe," said Lola.

"You're, welcome my love. Do you wanna talk about your day?" said the lady.

Lola said, "Not really."

The woman said, "OK. Well, do you want to take a bath?" Lola said, "I'll just take a shower."

The woman said, "OK. I'll run it for you."

Lola grabbed the lady by her arm as she sat up and said, "Not so fast. Today was just *crazy*. We found a man in a hotel room with a carrot shoved up his butt."

The woman said, "What? That's crazy."

The woman sitting on the couch with Lola was her significant other. One of Lola's biggest secrets was that she was a lesbian. She was afraid of what her family would think and of what her job would think if they knew that she was a woman who dated other women, because the guys on the police force would hit on Lola. They just thought that she was extremely masculine because she had such strength and mannerisms. Lola had a love for women ever since she was younger, and it just became harder to hide and doubt as she became an adult. She ultimately decided that she wanted to date women, so she discreetly did what she needed to do to experience that part of life, and it became a more comfortable lifestyle. After living life and experiencing heartbreaks as a result of herself and others, she and the woman sitting on the couch with her dated and eventually decided to build a life together. This woman was slightly older than Lola and nowhere near as adventurous, but they made it work for them. The woman's name was Scarlett. They lived a very simple, but fulfilling life with each other.

Scarlett looked at Lola and said, "Well, I'm sorry you had a hard day, but I'll do whatever I can to make it better."

Lola leaned into Scarlett and said, "As you always do. That's why I love you."

Scarlett said, "I love you too, babe."

Lola shook her head from side to side, looked at Scarlett and said, "You know what's crazy about the whole situation?"

Scarlett said, "No. What is it?"

Lola said, "I'm pretty sure that Blac had something to do with it."

Scarlett looked at Lola and said, "The third piece to our wonderful union."

Lola said, "Babe, this woman is ruthless. I mean, don't get in her way, 'cause she don't have any filters or understanding of the value of life when she ready to get you outta here. Like, I mean, *crazy*. They are *crazy*. I just can't believe that I got another case of hers. I'm just hoping that something happens to give me a break so I can actually build something against this woman, 'cause I'm quite sick of her, and I know everybody else is, too."

Scarlett wrapped her arms around Lola's shoulder and said, "Babe."

Lola looked at Scarlett with puppy dog eyes and said, "Yes?" Scarlett said, "Babe, you're home now.

Lola closed her eyes and said, "I get it. OK, I don't wanna talk about it anymore. How was your day? Did you get much work done today?"

Scarlett looked at Lola, unraveled her body, moved Lola's arm from around her shoulders and said, "Yes, I did get some work done today. But I don't wanna talk about that either," as she leaned in to kiss Lola yet again.

Lola kissed Scarlett back several times and said, "I understand what you want, and trust me, I want it just as bad." She stood up and said, "Let me take a shower."

Scarlett lay back on the couch and said, "I'll be waiting for you."

Lola left the room and headed into the bathroom. She turned on the water, and while she undressed and waited for the water to get warm enough for her to enter the shower, she couldn't help but think to herself about what she had seen earlier that day. *There was nothing he could have done that was so bad that he needed to be killed in that manner.* The visual of the deceased man in the room left a stain on her mind and heart. Lola's heart went out to the victim and those close to him. She never understood the philosophy or the reasoning behind these senseless murders, which was why she became a detective to begin with.

After thinking deeply, Lola shook her head, snapped out of her thoughts, finished undressing and got in the shower. The bathroom filled with steam as Lola tilted her head back, letting the water run down her face, removing all of the trauma that she had experienced from her job that day, just as she would do any other day. The bathroom door opened and horny Scarlett walked in and undressed herself. Lola wasn't paying attention, but she would become attentive within seconds of Scarlett pulling back the curtain and jumping in the shower with her. Lola wiped her face with her left hand and turned to face a beautiful, naked Scarlett as mist from the water hit both of their naked bodies. Lola leaned into Scarlett, not giving her much room to breathe and said, "Well, hello, beautiful." Scarlett, in a cute, flirty voice, said, "Hey, babe."

Scarlett massaged Lola's breasts, then began stroking her finger in a circular motion around Lola's areolas. Lola stood in a dominant stance with both of her arms by her sides. Biting her bottom lip, she lifted her left arm, which was closest to the shower wall, and wrapped her hand around Scarlett's neck, semi-aggressively pushing Scarlett toward the back of the shower. Lola placed her right hand above Scarlett's head and sunk her teeth into Scarlett's neck, then began sucking on the bite mark to soothe the pain.

Scarlett screamed out, "Ah!" followed by a sexy moan. Lola took both of Scarlett's arms, held them high over her head and slammed them against the wall of the shower. Scarlett closed her eyes and moaned as Lola went back to sucking on her neck. Scarlett slithered like a snake through sand and moved as much as she could, but Lola had her jaw locked on Scarlett's neck. Lola was consistent with Scarlett's movements and didn't lose her grip. Scarlett's moans became louder and louder as she was enjoying the passionate aggression that Lola was giving her. Lola released Scarlett's neck and proceeded to travel to other parts of her body, kissing and sucking other intimate areas.

Lola had gotten all the way to Scarlett's belly button, then came up and began very intimately kissing her lips while water splashed the tops of their heads and ran down their bodies. Lola picked up Scarlett and Scarlett wrapped her legs around Lola's waist. Lola carried Scarlett out of the bathroom and into the bedroom, gently laying her across the bed. She began sucking Scarlett's breasts; Scarlett moaned louder and louder and became more and more theatrical in response, arching her back and biting her lip. Lola worked her way down, kissing and caressing Scarlett's body. Scarlett was driven crazy by this enjoyment and pleasure, stroking her hands through Lola's head and pushing her down toward her happy place.

Scarlett was ready for Lola to taste her rainbow and suck up her lady juices, but Lola controlled the motion of this ocean, and she was going to show it by taking her time and forcing Scarlett to enjoy the pleasure. Lola dropped down to her knees, pried Scarlett's thighs apart from each other and slipped her tongue in between them. Lola kissed and sucked on Scarlett's clitoris and surrounding areas until Scarlett's body became weak and she was no longer able to control herself. Scarlett moaned even louder and screamed out, "My love! My love! My love! I love you, I love you, I love you! Oh, yeah! Oh, yeah! Oh, yeah!"

This turned Lola on and made her want to stroke Scarlett's clitoris with the tip of her tongue in up-and-down motions, stimulating it. Lola's head went up and down as if she was eating an ice cream cone. Scarlett clutched the sheets until she couldn't take it anymore and reached her hands down to stop Lola from devouring her, but that didn't work. Lola lifted Scarlett's body up, pinned her arms to her sides and went back down on her, quickly stroking Scarlett's clitoris up and down with her tongue. Scarlett screamed and moaned so loudly that the dog began to bark and cry. Not to worry, though; the dog was fine. Scarlett was also fine—*so* fine that after minutes of screaming, moaning and gasping, she started pushing back and rolling her hips in a circular motion, practically feeding her clit to Lola. Her vagina became wetter as her excitement rose, causing juices to go up Lola's nose and all over her mouth. Lola stood up and wiped her face with her hand, while a relieved Scarlett swallowed her spit and opened her eyes. In a split second, Scarlett's mouth opened and a loud moan of "Yesssss" sung through her lips because Lola had gone back in for seconds. This time, Lola used her index and middle fingers to stimulate Scarlett's clitoris while pushing her tongue in and out of her vagina. Scarlett started clutching the sheets again and even looked down at Lola as she worked. Scarlett sat up again, rolling her hips and riding Lola's tongue.

In a cute, purring voice, Scarlett yelled out, "I'm coming!" Her eyes rolled back, her body shook and a secretion came out of her.

Lola came up for air and said, "Oh, yeah, I love it when you come." She took her fingers and put them into her mouth, then leaned in to be face-to-face with a weak Scarlett. "Yummy. I love the way you taste," she said.

Scarlett, barely opening her eyes, said, "I love you."

They kissed each other on the lips and Lola got off of Scarlett, lying beside her. Scarlett turned over and got on top of Lola—she wasn't done. Scarlett straddled her legs across Lola's body. Lola leaned back, gripping both of Scarlett's hips while Scarlett kissed her neck, making her way to her breasts and sucking on her nipples. Lola squinted her eyes tightly while biting her lips and saying, "Damn, bae." Scarlett lifted her head, swinging her hair and grabbing her own breasts. She rolled her hips from side to side and up and down, massaging both of their vaginas together. As the tribbing intensified,

154

Lola begin to control the motions, lying on her back while Scarlett rode on top. Lola yelled out, "Oh, shit!" while Scarlett screamed, "Baby, I'm coming!" They both climaxed and Scarlett fell into Lola's armpit. Scarlett lay next to Lola, catching her breath. The two of them lay in satisfaction and fell into a deep sleep.

Lola and Scarlett weren't the only ones in the city who were engaging in some one-on-one lady time. Blac had a thing for the ladies, and she had no problem showing it and living it. In a suburban neighborhood, where one of Blac's infamous bachelorette pads was located, was the Boss. Blac had this specific residence decorated in a black and hot pink color scheme, and everything was cute. In a bedroom that had a black diamond platform bed with black silk sheets and hot pink pillows was a short, chocolate-colored woman. This woman was dancing around a stripper pole. The woman stood at five feet, three inches, and wore her hair long, all the way down to her butt. She was completely naked and wore nothing but stripper heels; she had breasts that sat up on her chest without a bra, a flat stomach and a nice, round butt. She had a pretty face with exotic features, she wore really long lashes and her makeup was done really well. Blac enjoyed the entertainment as she drank a homemade margarita, smoked a hookah that sat on the nightstand and lay in her bed wearing only a black diamond-studded corset top. This is how the Queen detoxed and relaxed.

Blac loved women, as previously stated, but she *loved* chocolate women the most. While she didn't discriminate, if she had to choose, she would choose chocolate. The young lady dancing went by the name of Mink; she was a longtime playmate—or girlfriend—of Blac's. For three years at this point, Blac and Mink had a situation in which Mink gave Blac companionship and loyalty, and in return, she was taken care of very well. Mink was usually not in the spotlight, but don't get it twisted—she wasn't too far behind, either. One night of fun had flourished into something a little more special, so she spent most of her time with Blac. Blac didn't have many obligations outside of Charlie, and she made that very clear, but Mink had a designated spot in Blac's mind. While that wasn't enough to stop Blac from venturing off and having interest in other women, they didn't hold a candle to Mink. There was just something about Mink that drove Blac crazy, and it showed every time they got together. Blac played soft music as she enjoyed the striptease that her little baby had been putting on for her and began to loosen the top of her corset. She lifted her breasts to her chin with her hands and rubbed her areolas with her thumbs as she closed her eyes. Mink took this as an invitation to come to the bed. Mink arched her back, sticking out her butt as she crawled onto the bed until she was able to get up onto her feet, then stood over Blac's head. Blac opened her eyes and looked at Mink as she squatted down and put her vagina in Blac's face.

Blac slid her body under Mink. Mink grabbed the top of the headboard and began riding Blac's face, rocking her body back and forth and stroking her clitoris against Blac's face and nose while Blac sucked the juices out of her vagina. Mink thrusted her clitoris into Blac's mouth, almost causing Blac to bump her teeth against the tip of her clit. Blac imprinted her hands on Mink's inner thighs and peeled her lips apart, where a pink clit poked out, and Blac began stroking the tip of her tongue against Mink's clitoris again. Mink looked back and reached one of her arms behind her. She slapped one of Blac's thighs and Blac opened her legs. Mink took two of her fingers and inserted them inside of Blac's vagina while stroking her clitoris with her bedazzled thumb. Mink continued playing with Blac while riding her face. This felt so good to Mink and she felt electric shocks throughout her body every time she thrusted forward. Mink began to have an orgasm, so she put both her hands on the bed in front of her body. She screamed and moaned until she fell onto Blac's face. Blac screamed, "I can't breathe!"

Blac frantically smacked her hands on Mink's thighs. Mink looked down, saw that her lover was in panic and got up.

Blac said, "Damn! I almost died."

Mink said, "No. Correction: You almost drowned," as she laughed with arrogance.

Blac said, "Oh, you think that's funny?"

The two ladies were now both sitting at the center of the bed. Blac reached into the top drawer of the chest next to her bed. She pulled out three items—a pink glass dildo; a long, skinny vibrator and a thick, nine-and-a-half inch rubber cock—and threw them onto the bed. Blac looked at Mink and said, "Are you ready?

Mink said, "No." She yanked Blac's head back and started sticking her tongue down Blac's throat. As her tongue went skinny dipping in Blac's mouth full of saliva, Mink pushed Blac back. Blac threw her legs behind her head and her feet touched the headboard. Mink stuck the long, skinny vibrator into Blac's vagina, pushing it in and out as Blac's juice box overflowed onto the bed. Blac gripped her ankles and yelled out, "Don't stop! Don't stop!" Mink penetrated her harder and faster until she nutted all over the toy. She lay there for a second, then grabbed the rubber dildo and stuck it all the way to the back of her throat until she gagged on it. Blac covered the dildo with spit and then told Mink, "Come here."

Mink said, "How do you want me?"

Blac said, "On all fours."

Mink said, "All fours?"

Blac said, "All fours, and quickly."

Blac smacked Mink's naked bottom as she got into position. Mink crawled to the middle of the bed and arched her butt in the air. Blac raised herself up onto her knees as Mink lay in position, at the mercy of the suspense of what Blac was about to do. Blac took the head of the vibrator and stimulated Mink's clitoris with it.

"Ah!" Mink yelled, followed by a sexy laugh.

Blac laughed as well and said, "You like that, don't you?"

Mink moaned and said, "Yesss. I like that."

Blac said, "I knew you would, you freak."

Mink laughed and said, "I'm yo' freak."

Blac said, "Is that so?

Blac spread Mink's butt cheeks apart and let a thick piece of saliva come from her mouth, dripping down the center of Mink's butt. She squeezed Mink's cheeks together and shook her cheeks together, then smacked her butt as loudly as she could.

Mink said, "Ouch."

Blac said, "Shut up."

Blac put the vibrator back on Mink's clitoris while she gagged on the dildo, getting it nice and wet.

Blac said, "I'm 'bout to bust this thang open."

Mink said, "Yesssss."

Blac rubbed the wet dildo around Mink's vagina, then very slowly pushed it inside.

Mink clutched the sheets and screamed, "Shitttttt!" really loudly.

Blac laughed and said, "Shhh. You can take it," as she loosened up Mink's tight vagina with her nine-and-a-half inches. Mink began throwing her body back to ease the pain and reach her climax at the same time. Blac noticed this and began rubbing her thumb around Mink's butt hole.

Mink stopped and said, "You better not think about it."

Blac said, "Nah, gangster. You got it."

Blac started thrusting Mink's vagina harder with the dildo. At this time, the dildo was soaked with spit and Mink's lady juices, so it didn't hurt her as badly. She was actually enjoying it, rolling her body and making lots of noise. It was time to kick it up a notch. Blac grabbed the glass dildo and spit on it, lathering it up, and slowly stuck it in Mink's anus.

Mink yelled, "Shit! No!"

Blac laughed and said, "You better not push it out."

Mink tensed up her body, squinting her eyes really tight and stroking her vagina over the rubber dildo. As she moaned and moved, the glass dildo slipped deeper and deeper until all Blac could see was the end of it, which was shaped like a hook. At this point, Blac was turned on. She grabbed Mink's hand and made her take control of the rubber dildo, watching her while playing with her own vagina and talking dirty to Mink. Mink's movements intensified and her body began to shake. Blac moved Mink's hand and started pounding her vagina with the rubber dildo until she screamed and creamed. Mink fell onto the bed. Blac quickly pulled the glass out of her butt and then went into the bathroom to clean the toys with soap and warm water.

Mink screamed, "Bitch!"

Blac laughed and said, "You'll live."   Mink sat up in the bed, collecting herself.

Mink said, "I can go to sleep now?"

A sexy Blac, wearing a black silk robe, came out of the bathroom and said, "Well, go to sleep," as she put the clean dildo back in the chest drawer by the bed.

Mink grabbed the vibrator and said, "Don't stiff me."   Blac said, "What?" with a sneaky smirk on her face.

Mink said, "You know what I want. Or, at least, what I want to see."

Blac, with a smile on her face, dropped her robe on the floor and jumped onto the bed. Mink moved to create room, leaned her body over Blac's, and started reviving Blac's clitoris, making her juices seep onto the sheets. Blac rolled her hips and moaned, and within two minutes, she yelled out, "I'm coming!" Mink moved over as a clear and white waterfall came from Blac's vagina, making a big puddle in the middle of her bed.

Mink clapped and said, "It's crazy how you can do that like that, and so quickly."

Blac said, "It's a gift, my dear. It's a gift. Anyways, get that blanket over there and press 'stop' on that clock."

Mink got out of the bed and pressed stop on a clock that was on the shelf facing the bed, then grabbed the blanket and covered the puddle.

Mink said, "You still make movies for him?"

Blac said, "You still in my business?"

Mink said, "I wouldn't."

Blac said, "Let's not tonight."

Both ladies got underneath a comforter and Blac turned on the TV as they snuggled up to each other.

Mink said, "You're right. Plus, I know we got great footage."

Blac said, "Facts."

The two ladies enjoyed some late-night television before falling to sleep.

CHAPTER 12
FRIENDS OR FOES

On an afternoon, Blac and her two drivers were driving down a busy street. One of the drivers was, well, driving; he wore all black. The passenger was another man who wore all black as well. In the back of the limousine was Blac, who wore a tight-fitting pink dress that pushed up her breasts, along with a black blazer. She accessorized with white pearls and diamonds in her ears as well as around her neck and wrists. An undercover detective car pulled over Blac's limousine.

The driver looked in his rearview mirror and said, "What now?"

As the car came to a halt, Blac, while fixing her clothes, said, "We good."

The passenger said, "Always, Boss Lady. Right?" He sought confirmation from the driver.

The driver nodded and said, "Always," as he watched someone walk towards the vehicle. As you may already guessed, that "someone" wore black slacks, flat black dress shoes, a white button-down, a black blazer and a black holster that held her gun. That "someone" was Lola. She wore black glasses on her face and her hair was pulled back into a ponytail. She walked to the driver's side of the car, stopped at the rear and knocked on the window. Blac rolled her eyes and raised her eyebrows as she pressed the button to roll her window down.

Blac sat back, looked at Lola and said, "Ma'am, how can I help you?"

Lola said, "Good day, Miss Blac. My name is Lola. I have a couple of questions for you regarding your friend, Paul Dunbar."

161

Blac said, "Will I need my lawyer to answer these questions? And what makes you think me and Paul were friends?"

Lola said, "No, I have no reason to bring you in, so your bigtime attorney can continue with his day. And I assume that you and Mr. Dunbar were friends because when tracing his last moments, I found out that he was last seen in The Black Silhouette at a table with you. But you knew that, just like you knew that Paul was dead." Blac said, "It's a small world. I might have heard something about it."

Lola said, "I'm pretty sure of it. Miss Blac, can you tell me your where abouts on the morning after you all were at The Black Silhouette between... I don't know... the hours of 2 a.m. and 4 a.m.? Blac said, "Getting pinned to the headboard by my man." Lola said, "Is there anyone who can verify that, like your man?"

Blac said, "Good luck getting him to even look you in the face without an arrest warrant," laughing at Lola's request. "But I do know that my on-property security guard was there until 8 a.m.; maybe he can give you the confirmation you need, Miss Lola." Lola took off her glasses, leaned into the window and said, "Listen, Blac. I know you know more about Paul's death than you're saying, and I'm going to find a way to prove it."

Blac said, "Well, on that note, I'm going to end this conversation, just like I would if I was trying to get you in bed and your husband walked up. If you have anything else, please contact my lawyer. And good luck finding Paul's killer—you're gonna need it."

Lola said, "Sure thing." She put her glasses on, stood up, fixed her coat and said, "I'll be in touch, Blac." In a louder voice, she said, "OK, I'll look into your where abouts, and here's my card. Let me know if you have anything else that can help me." She stood there, holding a business card with her contact information on it. Blac said, "I bet you will." She rolled up her window and the car drove off.

Lola shook her head and put her card back in her wallet. Lola walked to her car got in and drove off as well.

CHAPTER 13
THE REWARD IS HIGHER THAN THE RISK

The next afternoon, Blac was sitting on the couch in Asia's living room. Asia had black velvet furniture with silver chrome tables. Her living room was painted pitch black, so it was hard to see people when they were in the living room, and all the lights were off. Asia walked into her home through her back door, singing and humming love songs. When she came into the dining area, she could see someone moving in the living room. She immediately pulled out her pistol and pointed it at the couch.

"Who are you?" Asia asked.

Blac showed her hands, which lit up the dark room with her diamonds on her hands and wrists.

"Relax. It's just me," said Blac.

Asia turned on the light and said, "Blac, you gonna get shot doing stuff like this."

Blac said, "No, *you* need to fix the security in your house. You got all this money and all this stuff you doing and you got bad security. Or, should I say, easy access to break into your house." Asia looked at Blac and said, "Not for a normal person." Blac said, "You act like the people who we deal with are normal. But anyways, I came to see you 'cause I haven't talked to you in a couple of days. I need you to go out of town."

Asia looked at Blac and said, "Out of town...where?"

Blac said, "I don't know and I don't care. I just need you to lay low for a while. That last situation is pretty sticky right now."

Asia said, "What do you mean?"

Blac said, "I just want to make sure you're safe, and the only way to assure that you're safe is to make sure you're out of the way for a couple of days. Maybe a couple of weeks. I'll let you know when it's safe to come back."

Asia said, "I'm not running from nobody."

Blac said, "Here you go with this macho man attitude. This is not about you running. This is about you being the only person or the only thing that can tie me to Paul's murder. I got this nosy chick who came out of nowhere well not really nowhere but I don't know who she is, but for some reason, she's up my ass like a thong, so I need you to go away."

Asia looked at Blac and said, "I can't."

In Asia's mind, she couldn't leave because she did exactly what Blac told her to do. She found something to do and had occupied her time with it, and she found it unfair that she was now expected to just drop it and run off. Blac wanted her to find something outside of this role to focus on so that she could eventually fade into the background or leave the life altogether. So, now, Blac was telling her that the only thing that could distract her from this role was to leave because things had gotten real, as if they hadn't ever before. Asia wasn't cool with that.

Asia looked at Blac and said, "Well, I'm not running from you, whoever this chick is or nobody else. I got a man and I'm not leaving my man to satisfy whatever y'all got going on. We know how this works. I do my part and you do yours. I don't know what to tell you, 'cause I'm not leaving."

Blac put her hand on her right cheek, shook her head, rolled her eyes and said, "Asia, *please* don't tell me it's the musician."
Asia looked down as she twirled her finger on the table. She looked at Blac and said, "What if it is?"

Blac laughed and said, "You always been different. I figured you would have a different type of like or interest. Just make sure that he's right for you because, I don't know, he's not from our world."

Asia said, "Well, like you always make sure to remind me: I'm not, either, other than what you put into me. Remember?" Blac

164

said, "Yeah, but you had a natural finesse about you. I don't think he has it. He's a square."

Asia said, "Good, so then it will be no problem when it's time for me to completely walk away."

Blac said, "He really beat yo' drum and got yo nose open. Let me catch you before you float out of here on a love high."

Asia said, "Stop picking on me. I really like him. We've been spending a lot of time together. He listens. He doesn't judge me; he really just *listens*. I've never met a man who knew completely what I do and didn't judge me. And you know he wanna have sex—every man wanna have sex. But this is different. He's so much more in tune with who I am, and what I'm thinking, and how I feel, and how I look at situations, and how I receive different stuff and what I would do in different situations. It's like he really cares about me, and I think I care about him, too. I really, really like him."

Blac looked at Asia and said, "I'm happy for you. I've never been the type to block love, 'cause that's what I thrive off of. I love my Charlie. But just make sure that you're being careful and that you're separating your work life from your love life, 'cause that's where my mistake came in. That's my issue. And some of the trauma that I go through being who I am wouldn't be as bad if I had separated my love life from my work life. You have that luxury because of the type of person you're dealing with. Make sure you stick to that."

Asia said, "Duly noted."

Blac stood up and said, "Well, you have my blessing, and like always, I respect your mind. So, we'll do what we need to do as far as this Lola chick goes. If you have any issues, you let me know and I'll see you soon."

Asia looked at Blac and said, "Sooner than you realize." Blac gathered her things before she and her driver drove off into the night.

A band's lead singer sang as people walked into an energetic evening at The Black Silhouette. The club was jam-packed with people; there were men and women dressed in their finest outfits with lights, cameras and enjoyment everywhere. People were laughing, talking and singing everywhere. At a table at the very front of the club was—you guessed it—Blac. A male with a black pants and a white shirt walked around with a white cloth and a bottle of champagne, filling up every glass at the table. Blac laughed and talked with three different gentlemen. This had become a regimen of hers when she went to this club. She was conversing and enjoying her night, seeing all the beautiful young men and women who were entering the club. An unwanted guest walked up to her table wearing a long black trench coat, black slacks and a white T-shirt with her hair slicked back into a ponytail. Beneath her jacket was her black holster that held her service gun. This unwanted guest was Lola. Lola walked up to the table and said, "Good evening."

Blac looked at Lola and said, "I thought that I wouldn't hear from you, considering that my lawyer hasn't given me a call."

Lola said, "This is such a beautiful club with so many beautiful people in here! Why you wanna start with ugly stuff? 'Hello, how you doing?' would be an appropriate greeting, don't you think?"

Blac looked at Lola and said, "No."

Lola said, "Why you so mean to me?"

Blac said, "Why do you keep bothering me?"

Lola said, "I haven't even said anything. All I said was hello." Blac said, "Your presence bothers me. This is a nightclub. And I'm pretty sure your presence alone spooks a lot of people." Lola said, "If they're not doing anything illegal, then they shouldn't be worried."

Blac said, "That's BS and you and I both know it. What do you want, Lola?"

Lola said, "To let you know that we're still working diligently on the case and I'm watching your every move. So, watch what you do and who you do it with, because make one slip-up and I'll have you."

Blac raised both of her hands and shook them from left to right, saying, "Oooh, I'm so scared. I don't know if I should be turned on or freaked out."

Lola said, "Please be freaked out, because the other one makes me very uncomfortable."

Blac said, "You ever heard of free speech? I can say what I want."

Lola said, "I didn't detain you. I just said it makes me uncomfortable."

Blac said, "What's uncomfortable is the fact that you keep popping up in places where you think I'm at, yet you don't have any solid evidence to actually detain me."

Lola said, "Soon. I just wanted to make my presence known and let you know that I'm watching you."

Blac said, "You're one of many. Get in line. But if there's nothing else, I'm gonna say goodnight to you, 'cause you're making my table nervous and we want to enjoy our evening. OK?"

Lola said, "Sure," as she turned her back to the table. "Goodnight."

Blac rolled her eyes and Lola left the club.

A big chocolate man, wearing a yellow suit with a black shirt and black shoes, walked up to the table and said, "We need to talk, Blac. Blac put out her cigar and looked up at the man who was standing over her with his shiny white teeth, curly black hair and beady eyes.

Blac looked at the man and said, "Bruce, please have a seat." He walked up to the gentleman sitting across from Blac. Blac gave the seated man a deep stare and nodded, indicating that he should get up, and he did. Bruce looked the gentleman up and down, fixed this coat and sat down.

"Don't mind if I do, Miss Blac," he said.

Blac laughed and said, "Bruce, you are quite the character. Why so formal?"

Bruce leaned into the table, putting both elbows on the table. Blac looked at him and said, "Oh. Where's your table manners? You know you not supposed to put your elbows on a table."

Bruce said, "That's a dinner table. This is a goddamn club." Blac looked at him with a shocked face and said, "Who pooped in your Cheerios?"

Bruce sat back and said, "Nobody pooped in my Cheerios, but I'm quite sick of this 14 percent that I keep having to give you and your people."

Blac looked confused and said, "I mean, I don't follow. It's business. We take good care of you."

Bruce said, "I can take good care of myself; that's not the point. The point is that I'm making money, but I will make more if we cut the 14 percent down to, I don't know, seven."

Blac said, Wait, wait, wait, wait, wait, wait. You want me to cut your percentage down by half, when I got other people who pay 40 while you have been paying 14 and don't have a problem with it? I think you guys live really good and that with the risks that come with your situations, we deserve more. But we try to be fair, and everybody else seems to think we're fair, but you got a problem." Bruce said, "Everybody else kisses your ass and I don't." Blac said, "Agreed. But I'm not cutting 14 percent. Now, we can take half of your services away and then you can pay seven percent."

Bruce said, "That's not gonna work for me because I feel that seven percent is appropriate for what you guys offer."

Blac said, "No, it's not, and I don't even understand the fact that you are even bringing this to me. We have a legal binding contract with you."

Bruce said, "Give me a break. Y'all basically pimps and hoes, but you wanna legitimize it and charge fees. So, to hell with your contract. That contract don't mean nothing to me."

Blac said, "We are who we are and that's your first mistake. But I mean, you didn't do a drop this week, so right now, my 14 percent is being held up. So, as far as I'm concerned, me and you ain't got nothing to talk about."

Bruce said, "Well, I'm gonna go back to enjoying my night. You keep waiting on that 14 percent."

Blac said, "It's your world. I just live in it."

Bo walked up to the table as Bruce was leaving. He looked at Bruce and said, "Hey. I've been looking for you."

Bruce looked at Bo and said, "You ain't been looking for me."

Bo said, "But I was. Don't you got something for me?" Blac put her hand up and said, "Bo, don't worry about it. Bruce is taken care of; I took care of Bruce."

Now, Bruce was an out-of-towner, so he had never seen Blac in her rare form—actually, no one had. Blac had a very cool, calm and collected way of conducting her business and herself, especially when she had an audience, so no one took things too seriously when she was involved. Blac attacked so quietly that her opponents would never see the attacks coming, and this situation was no different in handling business. In the beginning, Bruce made $30,000 a week; now, he was making $1.5 million to $2 million a week. He started out needing protection, guidance and clientele for his fleet of ladies and somebody connected him with Blac.

She gave him all the information that he would need in order to be successful. So, him wanting Blac to change the amount that she charged him for her services was like a slap in the face to her. When he didn't make as much money, he was OK with paying the 14 percent, which was still far less than other clients were required to pay. But we all know that when you inquire more, you require more, and this may have caused Bruce to go from humble to greedy. This was dangerous for everyone involved. Blac was calculated and knew to step in before Bo got involved and things got messy and ugly. Blac knew the level of loyalty and love that her guys possessed. Bo allowed Bruce to leave the area as Blac sat with not a care in the world. Across the room sitting at the bar was a bubbly Asia, who wore a red dress with red lipstick and red pumps to match her rosy red, blushing cheeks. She wore her hair curly, as usual, and positioned her body in a way that allowed her to have a direct view of the band.

Asia was overfilled with joy because for the first time in a long time, someone was feeding her mind and soul. The man who made her bubbly was playing the saxophone on the stage. In between songs and sets, you could catch them giving each other flirty eyes and vibes. She enjoyed the music while drinking a double shot of cognac with three ice cubes and two cherries. In addition to enjoying her night, she was still on alert and on the lookout for her prey. Asia knew that it was a possibility that somebody would be on the feasting table tonight; she just waited for the chef to serve her plate. She was ready to put her next victim where they needed to be. Asia's phone dinged and she received a text from the Boss Lady. The text read a black heart. This signal was different—this was a very serious situation that had to be handled instantly and carefully. Asia knew that they were all being watched, so she had no intention of bringing any extra attention to herself or anyone else.

So, she took a different approach with Bruce than she did with Paul. With Paul, she owned everyone's attention and made sure that everyone in the room respected who she was and her femininity. This new situation was different because Bruce was a pimp, so he was always looking for a new girl. He was high-class, but nevertheless, he was a pimp. Asia figured that it would be easier to get his attention intimately than it would be to do so publicly due to the delicacy of the situation, Blac's life and her own life. Asia continued to enjoy her drink and enjoy the music of her beloved, and when she saw Bruce walk by, she followed him to the bathroom. This was a dangerous situation, but she shook off her fears and remembered that she was still on a job. She stood on the other side of the door as people walked in and out of the restroom. When she saw him coming out of the gentlemen's room, she walked out in front of him, cutting his walk path off. He nearly bumped into her, but stopped in just enough time.

Bruce stopped and said, "Damn, little mama. I almost knocked you over."

"I'm so sorry," said Asia. As she looked at him, he brought his body in front of hers and they were now face-to-face.

Bruce looked at her pretty face and said, "No, *I'm* sorry. I should've watched where I was going."

Asia stopped him and said, "No, it's my fault. I cut you off. I'm sorry; I just got a lot on my mind."

Bruce said, "What's wrong?" with a concerned look on his

face.

Asia said, "I just broke up with my ex. I thought I would come out here to have a drink or two, but I think I'm gonna head home because my mind is so messed up."

Bruce said, "There's a diner up the street. Would you like to get something to eat?"

Asia said, "No, I'm not really hungry. Plus, I've been drinking, and I don't wanna throw up."

Bruce said, "Well, let me walk you to your car."

Asia said, "It's too soon for me; I won't leave just yet."

Bruce said, "Can I just text you to make sure you get home safely? I won't harass you about spending time with you tonight, but I do want to make sure you're safe and you get home safe, because you do seem pretty distraught."

Asia said, "OK, I can do that," and pulled out her phone to store Bruce's number.

As Asia made some type of progress in her plan, trouble came around the corner. Trouble was a very sharply dressed and happy Jacob, who walked into the area where it had all started. This area held significant value, as it was the first real encounter he had with his beloved, but unfortunately, his beloved was by the bathroom talking to another man. The world instantly stopped, and so did the happy tune he was singing and humming. His happiness quickly disappeared and he was very shocked as he watched Asia. See, sometimes, we bite off more than we chew. While it sounds nice and cute when you tell someone that you are accepting of the flaws and traumas that come with them, you never really know what you're dealing with until you're truly faced with these flaws and traumas. Now, Jacob was aware of Asia's life and what she did, but to see her in action was surprising and a tad bit discouraging. This wasn't the first time he had seen her work, but something about this time really bothered him.

Asia felt really bad and followed Jacob onto the dance floor as he stormed out of the hallway. He stood at the doorway and said, "Asia, what are you doing?"

Bruce walked between the two of them, heading to the dance floor. Jacob looked at Bruce with a very stern look as he passed by. Bruce looked back at Jacob and laughed.

Asia pushed Jacob to get his attention, looked at him and said, "What's your deal? You know what I do. So, it's OK for me to tell you what I do, but it's not OK for you to see me in action? You act like this is something I hide from you. You're fully aware of what I'm doing and what I have to do."

Jacob said, "Well, why do you have to do it here?"

Asia said, "Newsflash: I was doing it here before me and you got close. Don't ruin a good thing because you're not being truthful about what you say you can endure and accept."

Jacob said, "I'm not judging you. I'm just a little bit taken back by it. I mean, when we first met, I could accept it because I didn't really know you; it was just, like, a fantasy. But now that we've gotten so close, I guess it's just hard for me to see something like that. But nah, I'm good. I got it."

Asia said, "I get it, but I need you to be strong. You say you accept my work, so I need you to relax."

Jacob said, "I just need you to be careful and not put it in my face."

Asia said, "I didn't put it in your face, and if I did, I'm sorry. I didn't mean to put it in your face. Let me fix it. Let me make it up to you."

Jacob said, "How are you gonna do that?"

Asia said, "You'll see," as she grabbed his hand and led him out of the club. They went back to Jacob's home.

CHAPTER 14
YOU COMING OR YOU AIN'T?

Jacob opened the door to his house with great confidence and class. At this point, his anticipation had calmed, and he was ready to conquer Asia's love. Asia and Jacob had been spending a lot of time together and, in a way, had become inseparable. While their conversations had fed each other's minds, it was interesting to see if their bodies would follow. Would Jacob be able to satisfy the sexual beast that Asia had been proven to be, or was he a silent killer who aimed to tame and make his women submit? Asia was certainly about to find out. Jacob held the door open for his lady while she walked in very slowly. Asia turned and looked at Jacob while he locked the door. Jacob walked toward her as she stood in the middle of his simple and modest living room. She looked around. His home wasn't over the top, but it was nice. The decor made it clear that Jacob was a man with class who didn't want to overdo things, and she enjoyed what she saw a lot. It gave her more confidence in him. Asia said to Jacob, "Hey, can I use your bathroom?"

Jacob said, "Of course you can, love." He placed his hand on the spine of Asia's back and escorted her to his powder room. "Take your time, love. I'll make us some wine. White or red?"

Asia said, "Red."

Jacob said, "OK," and left Asia to tend to her business.

Asia went into the bathroom and pulled her underwear down to her ankles. She was a little tipsy, and this made her ready to *go*. She closed her eyes as she used the bathroom, and as she finished, she let out a sexy moan and cleaned herself. She was ready. Asia's lady box was throbbing and sending shockwaves throughout her body. She looked down at her expensive underwear and realized that she had made a mess. Her panties were so wet that she could wring them out like a mop. Asia removed her clothes and walked out the restroom with them in her hands. By this time, Jacob was sitting on his couch. He had put white and pink roses all over the house, leading to the bedroom where soft music played and the flames of scented candles danced through the atmosphere. He had two glasses of red wine sitting on the table with a bouquet of white roses. Asia walked out wearing nothing but her heels and threw her clothes at his feet. Jacob looked at Asia and took a deep swallow.

Jacob said, "I got your wine," and stood up to hand her the glass.

Asia reached for the glass and said, "Thank you. Sorry 'bout the clothes. They got wet."

Jacob said, "You don't hear me complaining," while he tried to keep his eyes off of Asia's completely naked body. Jacob invited Asia to sit and she did. After about two glasses of wine a piece, Jacob couldn't take anymore. His mouth was watering and his mind was racing. Did she taste as good as she looked or smelled? Jacob was gonna find out, and *now*. Jacob dropped his body and planted his knees on the hardwood floor. He looked Asia in her face as he stroked his hand gently across her face. Asia bit her lip and stuck his fingers in her mouth. She sucked on two of his digits and let them fall out of her mouth, then closed his hand and held it up to her face. She closed her eyes and kissed the top of his hand. Jacob pulled Asia's body closer to him and lifted her legs all the way to the top part of the couch, where he had the perfect view of her beautiful vagina.

As her juices dripped onto his couch, he took his face and buried it in her vagina, licking and stimulating her clit. Asia moaned and moved, reaching for anything she could grab. Jacob pinned both of her legs to the back of her head and started rubbing his fat tongue up and down in a sloppy way, working his tongue from her clitoris to her ass. Jacob continued to feast as Asia screamed and moaned at the top of lungs. Jacob couldn't believe how theatrical and into it she was; this turned him on. Asia climaxed and shook.

174

Jacob stood up as Asia dropped to her knees, swallowing him whole. Asia penetrated the back of her mouth with Jacob's big shaft. She continued to dominate Jacob while giving him head until his legs felt weak. Jacob picked up Asia's face and looked her dead in the eyes with a deep passionate stare. Asia got lost in Jacob's eyes and began to melt. Jacob picked up Asia, wrapping her legs around his neck and licking all over her clit as he carried her to his bed. Asia hugged his head and moaned while rolling her eyes to the back of her head. The room was a lover's paradise, filled with roses, fruits, chocolate syrup and whipped cream. Jacob gently placed her on the bed. Asia turned to crawl to the head of the bed, but Jacob had different plans. He grabbed Asia by one of her ankles, pulling her close to him, Asia fell onto her stomach and Jacob began kissing and biting her back 'til he got to her butt. He took his belt and smacked her butt with it, creating a loud sound effect—that *definitely* stung.

Asia screamed and Jacob said, "Shut up."

Jacob picked up the can of whip cream as he watched this beauty slither and moan. He spread her butt cheeks apart, sprayed the whipped cream in her ass and started slurping it up. Asia held her breath, closed her eyes and made a cat-like moaning noise. Jacob ate all of the dairy whipped cream from her darier until it was gone and she couldn't take it anymore. He stood up, took a strawberry out of the tray and bit it. Jacob grabbed Asia by her neck and kissed her deep in her mouth, transferring the fruit from his mouth to hers. Asia chewed and swallowed the strawberry, then arched her back and slid her body to the edge of the bed where Jacob was standing. Jacob said, "Come on, Mama. Get it."

Asia thrust her vagina up and down on his stick throwing her body back at him and riding and taking electric back shots, as Jacob enjoyed the view and stroked his nails down her arched back, making her vagina become wetter and wetter as she climaxed. Jacob smacked her ass, we walked around to the top if the bed and lay in the bed. Jacob's pole stood up in the air like a third leg. Asia got on top of Jacob and squatted with both of her feet planted. She started moving up and down on his penis, using the bed for balance, while grabbing her breast. Jacob grunted and twirled his toes 'til cum oozed out of his meat. He took it out and wiped it on her clit. Asia got up to wipe it off, and when she came back, Jacob was sitting butt naked in a chair, playing with his meat. Asia walked up to him and shoved his meat down her throat 'til she gagged on it. She paced herself and consistently stroked the back of her throat with his stick. Soft music played to set the mood and Asia held onto the back of the chair while passionately moving her hips in a circular motion, drowning his penis in her lady juices. She leaned into Jacob as he buried his face in her breasts.

Asia moaned and said, "You like that?"

Jacob said, "Yeah," as he thrust his body forward, forcing himself deeper into Asia. She wrapped her arms around his head as she felt the shock of every movement he did. Asia's body shook as she held him tight as he went faster and deeper inside her to climax. Asia got off of him and then in a sexy defeated strut walked her naked body and bouncy booty to the bed and lay on the bed. Jacob followed her with not only his eyes but his body too and laid behind her, cuddling her from behind. Asia wiggled and moved 'til Jacob's penis was between her butt cheeks. Jacob placed his palm on the lower part of Asia's spine and Asia arched her back as Jacob inserted himself into her ocean. Asia went back to moaning and screaming as she threw her ass against his stomach as their bodies intensely intertwined and they made passionate love. As a threw her head back and looked at Jacob from over her shoulder as their faces met and they deploy and passionately kisses each other. Asia opened her legs exposing her pretty little twat as Jacob continued to kiss her while reaching his hand across her body to very sensual and gently rub her exposed genital area. This turned Asia on ever more she closed her eyes really tight yet again moaning and throwing her body back at Jacob.

This fired up the mode a little bit more Jacob grabbed a patch of Asia's hair as a loud "Fuck" projected from his mouth. He had basically put Asia in a headlock, and she didn't move as Jacob became more of a sexual beast, He got on top of Asia and spread

176

her legs apart as far as they could go. Then, while standing on the bed, he started drilling her vagina with his tool. Asia screamed and yelled, as he was applying great pressure to her ,then he let her legs go and put his body on top of hers in an flat position swirling in a circle while gripping her butt, Asia moaned, gasped for breath as she came and orgasm. He kissed her on the mouth and changed positions. Jacob laid in the bed as Asia began kissing all over his body until she met his one-eyed monster again. She spit on the top of it and slid her mouth down until her eyebrows touched his pubic hairs, then continued pushing it in and out gagging and choking for several minutes, Jacob clutched the sheets, then grabbed the back of her head.

"Catch it." Jacob said in a demanding voice. Jacob nutted in Asia's mouth and she swallowed.

The next afternoon, Asia's phone rang. On the other side of it was a very upset and disappointed Blac. Asia woke up knowing that there was going to be an issue because she was not able to conquer what she was supposed to regarding Bruce. Asia gathered her thoughts, pondered the explanations she would give and went to the office to meet Blac. When she walked into Blac's office, she felt her energy, and it wasn't good. Blac stood in the window as the rain hit the open glass window; it was storming outside and the weather matched what was going on in Asia's world at the moment. Blac did not even budge when Angelica walked in to tell her that Asia was in the room. Angelica closed the door.

Blac, holding a sack of money in her hand and with her back still to Asia, said, "I knew this love interest would be an issue."

Asia looked at Blac with a confused look and said, "How do you figure?"

Blac turned, walked toward Asia and said, "I seen you leave last night. Now, call me crazy, but I was thinking that maybe you left to tell that boy what he needed to hear so that he could calm down and you could go on about your mission, but that's not what happened. I didn't get a phone call from you. I didn't get a text message from you. I didn't get anything from anybody indicating that this job was done, so I assumed that it wasn't! Now, was it?"

Asia said, "No, ma'am, I was not able to finish. But don't worry; I will get it finished."

Blac sat at her desk and said, "You better, and it better be done well, because from the day I met you, I have been doing everything you've asked of me and some of what you haven't. I thought we had an understanding that we would separate the two so that it would not be an issue and this person would not interrupt what you have going on work-wise. By all means, I'm for it. I love the fact that you're actually happy. I love the fact that you're doing something outside of this. I love the fact that you're actually venturing off and understanding that there's a life outside of this and that this can end at any moment. But while you're still in, you need to be focused and you need to make sure that you're doing what's necessary." Asia said, "Out of all the things I've done, this is the one time when it's taking me a little bit longer to get things done, and you're making me feel bad about it. I'm actually confused, because one minute, you want me to find something to do to occupy my time, and then, when I do, it's a problem."

Blac stopped Asia and said, "Wait right there. You will *not* make me out to be the bad person in this situation. You do your part and I do mine. You agreed to this understanding years ago. You and I both understand what needs to be done, and don't make this about the little saxophone boy—this has nothing to do with him. This is all about you and you not being able to focus on what you need to focus on. Don't make it seem like I'm badgering you or trying to downplay your relationship, 'cause I'm notable for chewing bubble gum and walking at the same time. I love Charlie, but I never let Charlie interfere with my work as much as he may want to and as much as he tries. I do what's necessary for my work because I have an obligation to you girls and to everybody on my team. And, my love, we have an obligation to each other. I asked you before you took this job if it was going to be a problem and you told me no, but this guy is a problem because he's stopping you from being able to successfully do your job. I have a problem with that."

178

Asia looked at Blac and said, "Before you think or say anything else, I'm gonna tell you right now that this is not a problem and that I am going to do what I need to in order to fix this."

Blac looked at Asia and said, "You better."

Asia grabbed her stuff and left the room. This interaction upset her a lot, but she understood that it wasn't personal—this was business. Or… was Blac becoming jealous or intimidated by the fact that Asia was actually doing what she asked her to do by moving on? Or… was she just worried about her being able to do what she needed her to do? Who knows? Anyhow, Asia knew that she had an obligation to take care of, so she planned on fixing the situation. Asia knew that there were pros and cons to the way her life was now. Pro: she had just encountered one of the most prolific, eye- and nose-opening intimate encounters that she had ever had, and it wasn't attached to business or dead white men printed on paper. This was different. This was new.

This was way too good to be true, because she believed that she was not worthy of being loved due to what she did. She couldn't help but believe that, because in society, people are taught that people who proudly live in their truth should be shamed or targeted while fairytales and people who pretend to be something they're not are glorified and idolized. While this may be silly or pompous, most of us who do this tend to accept the responsibility of being outcast and ridiculed because we wear the hate from others like badges of honor. Asia was no different. As proud and open she was, it didn't stop her from having thoughts that no one would accept her because of who she truly was and what she did. These were the thoughts that went through Asia's head. She leveled with herself, picking apart her heart while considering her mind and trying to balance both. This was more of a task for Asia than she thought it would be, as this was a new part of life that she hadn't experienced. While she knew what she was feeling and she definitely knew what she needed to do, she had to figure out how to show love and loyalty to both Blac and Jacob—or did she? Maybe it was time to step into her divine new destiny, where she was not judged for her past but instead working toward a fulfilling future. Well, the reality of the situation was that Blac was furious and disappointed, which Asia was not used to. Asia knew that she may want to drive off into the sunset with her Romeo, but she couldn't yet. So, back to business as usual.

CHAPTER 15
STAY READY SO YOU AIN'T GOTTA GET READY

Asia went to a big brick house that reminded her of a school.

She rang a really loud doorbell and a voice said, "Who is it?"

Asia pressed the button and said, "It's yo' Aunt Mary."

The voice said, "Come on in, Aunt Mary!" The door opened and Asia walked down a long hall that had a beautiful chandelier in the center and gorgeous brown marble floors. The walls were painted burgundy and decorated with expensive paintings. Asia walked into a room filled with shades of brown, burgundy and red and sat down on a nice, red antique couch. Asia was dropping by to visit Nicole and catch up.

Don't get me wrong, they did chat often but somethings just had to be said face to face, this was more than just a friendly conversation. In the middle of the conversation, Asia looked at Nicole and said, "Hey, do you still see Bruce from time to time?" Nicole rolled her eyes and said, "Yes. He comes around like clockwork every week."

Asia said, "Really? So, do he come to you, or do you go to him?"

Nicole looked back at Asia, shrugged her shoulders and said, "It varies. Sometimes, I go see him just because he don't wanna travel. A lot of times, he comes to me just because he likes the suspense of not knowing what I might look like when he walks in. I usually dress up for him. Why you ask?"

Asia laughed and said, "He's on my plate."

Nicole shook her head and said, "I don't even wanna know how he ended up on your feasting table. But what I will say is that I have a date with him tomorrow night and it's at his place, so I don't know how you gon' swing that, but I'm pretty sure you'll figure something out. You're pretty clever."

Asia looked at Nicole, said, "I am…" and looked down. Nicole looked at Asia, her expression turning somber, and said, "What's wrong?"

Asia said, "I think I'm done."

Nicole said, "It took you long enough."

Asia said, "What do you mean?"

Nicole said, "I ain't gon' front. Me and Blac been talking about you getting out for a long time now. It's just that it was always your choice, so when you was ready was when you was gonna do it. And every time I ask her about it or ask her if she talked to you about it, she would say you wasn't ready, and when you was, it would happen."

Asia looked at Nicole and said, "Tell me something."

Nicole looked at Asia and said, "No, I've never had sex with Blac."

Asia laughed and said, "No? Never? I was just curious. She's something else, so you never know."

Nicole said, "That she is. Everybody thinks that, but I look at Blac as more of like a big sister or one of my home girls that just knows about life because she experienced it. She's not somebody I want to sleep with. You don't understand how many arguments I've had in my relationships over this lady. They feel like me and her are too close and I slept with her, when the reality is, we ain't nowhere near as close as she is with the other girls, like you, for example. But because I like women and she likes women, they just assume that we have some type of unspoken relationship, when the reality is, Mink ain't going nowhere and Charlie knows that. But that woman changed my life."

Asia said, "Mines, too. Facts."

Nicole said, "I think that's so crazy because people don't

even realize that you and Blac are closer than me and Blac could ever be, but that's because I'm different."

Asia said, "You are who you are and we are who we are, and it's good that people don't know how close we are. That's the best thing for all of us."

Nicole agreed. "Yeah, but I'm ready to get out, too. 'Cause if *you* ready to get out, I know I should've *been* out. I've been doing this longer than you have and I'm ready to be a stay-at-home wife." Asia's eyes got big and she said, "Wife?!"

Nicole shook her head up and down and said, "Yes. I've been married for four years now."

Asian said, "You whore! Why you ain't tell anybody?"

Nicole said, "Blac came to the ceremony and everything." Asia said, "Blac knows *everything*. I'm offended. I thought we were better than that!"

Nicole said, "We are. It's not personal. I wanted to protect my spouse."

Asia said, "She OK with what you do?"

Nicole said, "Yes. Let me tell you something. When somebody truly loves you for who you are, there are certain sacrifices that they'll make when it comes to who you are and what you do. So, if you find somebody that's willing to make that sacrifice and do that, then that's something worth having. I don't care what nobody say."

Asia said, "Touché."

Nicole pulled the basket of clothes closer to her, started folding them and said, "But I'm starting to feel different about it, so I'm ready to get out. I got enough money to be a stay-at-home wife and fold clothes and cook for the rest of my life and never have to look at another shaft if I don't want to. The only shaft I want to look at is the ones they make in a sex shop, so I'm ready to get out."

Asia said, "I get it."

Nicole looked at her and said, "You do?"

Asia said, "Yeah, I do. I feel completely different. These last couples series of events in my life have been a change of energy for my universe." Nicole started laughing. "So, you mean to tell me, little Jacob changed your life?"

Asia stood up, rubbing her chest, and said, "Well, I ain't gon' brag, but ya might wanna stop calling him 'little Jacob.'"

Nicole leaned back on her couch, put her right hand over her chest and said, "OK. Jacob or *big* Jacob?"

Asia looked back at Nicole as she swung her hair and said, "Big Jacob is *Daddy* to me." Both ladies started laughing.

Nicole said, "OK, 'cause this is something I ain't never seen and I am loving every minute of it. I think it's important for everybody to have love, even us girls. At the end of the day, we're still people and our hearts throb like everybody else's, not just our vaginas."

Asia said, "You could say that ten more times! But I like him. He knows who I am and he knows what I do. All men are pigs, actually. So, basically, you know."

Nicole said, "You found your Mr. Right."

Asia looked at Nicole and said, "He's better than I hoped, so maybe I did."

Nicole looked at her and said, "I think so. And don't worry 'bout Blac. I'm pretty sure she is gonna be happy for you, long as you do it the right way."

Asia looked at Nicole and said, "What?"

Nicole looked at her and said, "Yeah. I heard what happened. I knew he was on your dinner plate before you told me. When she's pissed, she feels the need to call me. I don't know what it is; the lady crazy. But she definitely called me and told me what happened, and you definitely gotta fix it."

Asia sat on the arm of Nicole's sofa and said, "I know," as she crossed her arms and scrunched up her face.

Nicole looked at her and said, "I *know* you not pouting."

Asia said, "I'm just saying, she sends me mixed signals."

Nicole said, "Yeah, probably, but she means well. She wants what's best for you, and she do feel like you need something else to do, but not at her expense. So, if you truly wanna get out, finish the job and then finish your arrangement with Blac."

184

Asia uncrossed her arms as she received the message and accepted what she had to do next. She folded her hands in her lap and said, "I guess you're right."

Nicole said, "I'm always right. The world would be a much better place if everybody just listened to me. I tell my wife that all the time."

Asia stood up and said, "I don't have time for you. I hope to meet this wife of yours someday soon. But until then, call me when you on your way to Mr. Bruce's house. I got something for him." Nicole shook her head, started laughing and said, "I'm pretty sure you do. I'll be in touch soon."

Nicole stood up and came face-to-face with Asia. Asia gave Nicole a kiss on her forehead and headed towards the door.

As Asia left Nicole's house, she digested all of the things that were said regarding not only Blac, but Jacob as well. She was willing to change her old lifestyle for Jacob and she decided that this was already inevitable before she spoke to Nicole, but Nicole just confirmed everything she was thinking and feeling. So, she knew that this was possibly going to be her last job; she just didn't know how she was gonna break the news to Blac because they had built such a close and very lucrative relationship with the positions they played in each other's worlds. But she knew that this was best for her and she knew that it was time.

Asia went home, where she had multiple text messages and voicemails from Jacob. Jacob was put on punishment—not a bad punishment, but a little time-out. This was because he had gotten her in trouble with her business partner, and that's one thing Asia wasn't used to. She wasn't used to blurring lies between relationships and business, because her relationships were business and it was usually as simple as that. But this relationship wasn't a business one, so she had to figure out how she was going to balance the two. She knew that, priority-wise, she had to go handle Bruce. While driving Jacob's anxiety through the roof and making him question his bedroom skills, Asia started putting her pieces in place for her game of chess that would allow her easy access to him with a clean murder. Asia laid in her bed with her hair wraps and her feet propped up on her bed, watching TV and eating food while drinking chamomile tea that she had added honey and garlic to. This was one of many remedies that she used to keep her body hydrated and soothe her soul at the same time. She watched classic TV and got lost in her head and thoughts until she started to nod off. She put her tea and snacks on the table next to the bed, turned off the lights and the TV and snuggled up in her comfortable blanket. Off to sleep she went.

The doorbell rang and at the door was a sexy Nicole, wearing knee-high stockings, black leather shoes and an auburn trench coat that covered her nude lingerie. Bruce walked to the door wearing an open white button-down, black dress pants and all-black socks. He opened the door with a smile.

"Hello, beautiful," he said.

Nicole, standing in the doorway, ripped her coat open and said, "Hello, handsome. You miss me?"

Bruce smirked and said, "Of course," looking at her beautiful naked body standing in the doorway to his home. She didn't even ask him to move; she practically just pushed him out the way and entered his home.

"Well, come in," he said.

Nicole looked back at him and said, "I wasn't asking. I was coming in anyways."

He laughed and said, "Would you like a drink?"

She said, "No, thanks. Actually, I brought *you* a treat."

He said, "Oh, yeah?"

She said, "Yes. I know that you are a wine connoisseur, so I thought you would appreciate a bottle of 1929 Italian red."

He said, "A lady with taste. I like it."

Bruce grabbed the bottle, opened it and poured both of them a glass. Nicole took off her jacket, and spread it across the couch and sat down on top of it. This was her distinct and organized way of not leaving any handprints. Nicole had her own bottle of wine and glasses to accompany them, so no one would be able to trace her whereabouts and place her in his home. She was scary as hell, hence why she never was on that type of mission—at least, not leading it anyways. Her anxiety was a bit high because she knew what was coming, but she played it cool as she usually did. She always had roles in situations that involved Asia and Blac, but these roles were always minor one and she never left any traces of herself. She wasn't going into this situation any other way; she treated it as she would any other. Nicole sat down, laughing and talking with Bruce, but she made sure that she didn't touch anything in his house—and, more importantly, she tried not to touch *him*. But that sure didn't stop him from touching her. Bruce grabbed Nicole by her neck and started kissing on her breasts. She tilted her head back and rolled her eyes, knowing that something was coming next.

She sat the glasses on the table and said, "Take a drink. You not gonna waste this good ol' wine, are you?"

Bruce said, "No. I was just setting the mood."

Nicole said, "You're good at that, so I hear."

Nicole poured a little more wine in each of their glasses for each of them and they toasted to everlasting memories. Bruce continuously told her how beautiful she was and that he enjoyed every moment that they had spent with each other. He became one of Nicole's regulars and he felt the need to tell her that he was appreciative of her. She knew he was full of it, but she rolled with it because she knew it wouldn't be long. The stars aligned and Bruce had a phone call that he had to take. He looked at the call and said, "Baby, give me about two minutes. I gotta take this phone call."

As he picked up his phone and walked towards the back of the house, Nicole sat there, very still and timid. She was trying not to touch or leave her prints on anything other than what she planned on taking with her when she left. The timing couldn't be better. Nicole reached into her bra and pulled out a small capsule. She opened it, put it into Bruce's drink and swirled the glass around. She picked up her glass and started drinking; she had finished in the nick of time. Bruce reentered the room.

Bruce said, "Baby, I'm sorry. That was really important; I had to take it. Anyways, where were we?"

Nicole looked at Bruce and said, "You were gonna drink your glass, because I'm not gonna be the only one getting drunk tonight." He laughed and said, "You always being feisty."

She said, "I'm not being feisty. I'm just saying, I'm 'bout to be ready to go and you're gonna be sober."

Bruce said, "I think I perform well sober."

Nicole said, "I didn't say you didn't. Drink up."

Bruce sat back in the chair and said, "Yes, ma'am," as he gulped down the whole glass. Nicole didn't know why he would do such a thing, but he did, and it worked out in Nicole's favor. Nicole sat there as Bruce began to instantly get drowsy. She asked him what was wrong.

He said, "I don't know. I guess I got drunk too fast."

Nicole said, "Would you like some water?"

He said, "No, I'm OK. Where were we?" before falling down onto the ground in front of Nicole, just missing her feet.

"Wake up, sleepyhead," a voice standing over a now bonded, shirtless and tied-up Bruce said. Bruce's back was facing the front door while the beautiful Asia smacked him out of his sleep.

Bruce said, "Hey, what are you doing here? Where is Nicole? Why are you in my house?"

These were the questions that a now awake, albeit drowsy, Bruce said when he saw this beautiful, five-foot-seven, caramel skinned, curvy beauty standing over him. Her hair was curly and came to her shoulders, and she wore dark makeup with sexy lipstick that made her lips pop. She towered over him, wearing a black full body leather suit and black leather gloves. She circled around him. Asia said, "Relax. You don't sound happy to see me."

Bruce looked at Asia and said, "I'm never happy to see someone I didn't invite. And why am I tied up? What do you want from me? What are you doing here?"

Asia looked at Bruce, laughed and said, "Now, Bruce, you know who I am and you know *what* I am, so you know why I'm here."

Bruce looked into Asia's eyes and said, "I guess I'm looking into the eyes of death."

Asia shook her head up and down and said, "So, you *do* know who I am."

Bruce looked at Asia and said, "Everybody in the city knows who you are and what you do, but what do you want with me?"

Asia pushed his head and said, "Just like a man."

Bruce said, "Ouch. What was that for?"

Asia said, "You too busy thinking with yo' little head. Yo' big head can't catch up."

Bruce looked puzzled. He had no idea what Asia was getting at.

Asia slapped his head again.

Bruce said, "Stop, you crazy bitch!"

Asia said, "No, bitch. *You* crazy. You don't remember trying to take me out to eat at the Black Silhouette?"   Bruce looked as if he had seen a ghost.

Asia nodded her head up and down and said, "You're screwed. But before I raw dog you, What's your issue with Blac?"

Bruce laughed and said, "Y'all women trying to control a man's world is comical. Untie me before something bad happens to anybody. I don't wish that on you or your boss."

Asia pulled a sharp pocket knife out of her pocket, popped it open and put it against Bruce's neck.

"You not as smart as you look," she said. Bruce closed his eyes and exhaled as Asia put the knife to a delicate part of his neck. If she poked him hard enough, she would instantly kill him.

Asia leaned her pretty face towards his and said, "Now, what makes you think you're dealing with some rookies? You better wake up some more. I'm inside *your* house, uninvited, and you think you will be more of a threat to me?"

Asia stood back up, looking down at Bruce as he looked up at her with an uncomfortable expression. Asia walked away, from him strutting and flinging her hair. She spun around and looked at him.

"Now," she said, "let's recount the series of events that just occurred. You see one of your faves, who happens to be a really good friend of mine and who happens to work closely with your arch nemesis. You drink a drink and *boom*, you pass out. Now, you're tied up, she's nowhere to be found and I'm in your house, uninvited. And you know why I'm here, so you *know* it's about to happen. I shouldn't be afraid of you; you can't even control your own life, let alone somebody else's. You are a sorry excuse for somebody who's supposed to be the head of anything."

Bruce exhale and said, "I'm not worried about a thang. I've done everything and I done touched everything anyways." Asia looked at him and said, "Well, in that case, let me not waste your time."

Asia walked over to the door and opened it. Loud footsteps stomped, followed by the clacking of Asia's heels on Bruce's brown hardwood floors. A big Black man, dressed in a black long-sleeved shirt with a mask over his face, black pants and huge black boots, walked in with a black bag that looked like an oversized pillowcase. Whatever he had in the bag was uncomfortable; it made a very piercing noise and was moving around a lot. The man held the bag away from his body and had a tight grip on it.

The man walked in front of Bruce and said, "I need to feed it."

Asia said, "They hungry? They gotta have something to eat." Asia looked at the man who had just come and said, "Dude, relax! I got you covered."

Asia pulled out a jar of peanut butter and proceeded to spread peanut butter all over Bruce's body. Bruce yelled and screamed, insulting her while making noise.

The man with the mask said, "I hate to hear a grown man scream."

Asia said, "I know. You're a sexy screamer."

Bruce spit at Asia, just missing her.

Asia said, "I seen it in yo' face. I knew you was finna try it." She pulled out her phone and opened her music app. She played really loud music that had harsh, gritty, loud beats. The music drowned it out Bruce's yelling and screaming—at least, for the moment. Bruce

190

proceeded to insult Asia by calling her multiple names and telling her that she was nothing but a hoe. Asia was unfazed because she knew that he wasn't no saint either, so if she was a hoe, he was *definitely* 'bout to get fucked. And he ain't even have to pay—this one was on the house and she made sure of that. After she was done spreading the peanut butter all over Bruce's body, Asia stood up and walked out of the house. She stood on the front doorstep as the masked man opened the bag, releasing rats. The rats crawled all over Bruce's body; they began to eat him alive as he screamed and squealed. The masked man handed Asia the bag and she stuck the peanut butter jar inside of it. The two disappeared into the neighborhood, walking up the block to their black SUV before getting in and driving off.

They circled the block to see if anybody went towards the house or if anything out of the ordinary was happening on the street. Nothing seemed suspicious, so they left the area without any worries.

Down the street in the cut was a little gray car that was parked; inside was Jacob, pretending to read a newspaper. After the SUV passed, Jacob closed the paper and looked at the house. At this point, he was whipped, following his lady around when she was tryna handle business. Or, maybe, he cared about her and the relationship and was very determined to win his love over. And, maybe, in order to do that, he felt like he needed to know exactly what she was doing when she wasn't responding to him and putting him on the back burner. Well, they say love makes you do some strange thangs.

So, while she thought that she was fulfilling her obligation to Blac to be done with this mess, her beloved followed her and ended up at Bruce's residence. Jacob got out of his car and, in a very discreet manner, walked up to Bruce's door. The door was left open, so it wasn't hard for him to get in. When he walked in, he saw a very horrific scene—a man being eaten alive by rats—and it scared him. Jacob quickly ran out of the house and headed back to his car, dropping a tube of lipstick into the grass on his way to safety. He got in his car and quickly drove off. Jacob was very distraught and confused, but he now had found the answers he was looking for. The only other question was, what was he going to do with the information he had just learned about his beloved?

The day continued and everybody went on with their lives while Bruce's body began to decay and stink. Lola continued to drive herself crazy, constantly interviewing and questioning anybody who would talk to her regarding Paul Dunbar's murder. Asia, on the other hand, had a sense of relief knowing that she and Blac were back to being shoulder-to-shoulder with one another. More importantly, her last job was finished. Jacob was hurt, scared and confused, and he did things to occupy his time while he sorted through his thoughts. Now, Blac? She just did what she always did. Nothing really drastic was going on in her world—at least, that's what she would tell herself to get through.

Two days after Nicole's date at Bruce's house, one of Bruce's girls went to check in with him. She felt that she may have done something wrong and needed to patch things up. While she had no recall of a reason why she would be put on a time-out, she was definitely going to see, because with his mood swings, you could never be too sure.

A light-skinned, big booty girl with a flat stomach and blonde hair, wearing a highlighter yellow dress with mustard yellow and pink stilettos, pulled up to Bruce's residence. By this time, the wind had blown his front door shut and his house appeared peaceful from the outside.

The woman got out of the car, walked to his front door, pulled a napkin out—because COVID-19 is real—and opened his door with the napkin wrapped around the knob. Rats ran past her feet; she jumped and screamed. She walked into the house and saw the body of dead Bruce, causing her to let out a shriek.

The police, the fire department and paramedics all arrived at the scene shortly after the call came in. Soon, Lola and her partner arrived at the scene.

"What do we have here?" said Lola to the police officer.
The police officer said, "Same story. Man appeared to be eaten by rodents."

Lola said, "Excuse me?"

192

The officer said, "Yes, ma'am. Looks like he's been dead for about 48 hours, and he was found by a lady claiming to be his girlfriend. She said she usually talked to him every day, but hadn't heard from him. She thought he was mad at her, so she went to see what was up and saw that he had been eaten by rats. She was pretty shaken up. In other news, there are rodents all over the house, dead *and* alive."

Lola said, "This woman is getting out of hand."

Her partner looked at her and said, "You think it's Blac?" Lola said, "I know it's Blac. First, you got a man with the carrot stuck up his ass. Now, you have this. This woman is on a rampage and I'm not sure what the motive is, but I don't know of anybody else who could possibly be responsible."

The police officer said, "But she has no ties to any of these men."

Lola said, "But she does! All of these men are crooks. They're successful businessmen who live in the underworld, a place where she's very popular."

John said, "But can we put her with them?"

Lola thought and said, "We can't... or *can* we?"

Her partner said, "I don't know. Can we?"

Lola and her partner walked through the house while her partner wrote down the notes that the first responders had gathered at the scene. While it wasn't much, it was something.

The police officer looked at Lola and said, "I see no motive. It's not a break-in. No trauma other than him being tied up and, of course, his body being eaten by rodents. I looked for a container of peanut butter—nothing. Nowhere. House is wiped clean. I have nothing for you."

Lola said, "Well, whoever did it did it right."

The police officer said, "I would think so. Whoever did this knew exactly what they were doing and they didn't want any traces to be found."

A voice outside said, "Hey, I got something!"

The police officer and the two detectives walked out to the

lawn of Bruce's house.

"What you got?" the officer asked.

The gentleman who called them held something in an evidence bag and said, "Not much."

Lola pulled a tissue out of her pocket and said, "It's not much, but I'll take it." She looked at a police officer and said, "Do you have ballistics here?"

The police officer said, "Yes." He tapped a lady on the shoulder and said, "Hey, can you take this back? It's lipstick. See if you can get any handprints or anything that has any type of identity or DNA on it so that we can see who it belongs to. The woman nodded, took the bag and disappeared.

The police officer said, "It's not much and it doesn't prove they're the killer, but it may be something that can give us some leads."

Lola looked at the police officer and said, "Some news is better than no news. Well, thank you, officer. We really appreciate you for everything, but we'll take the investigation from here.

The officer said, "No problem. Good luck to you guys," and walked away from Lola and her partner.

John said, "We got our work cut out for us with this one, but hopefully that lipstick gives us a break. Do you think that lipstick belongs to Blac?"

Lola looked at him, laughed and said, "I highly doubt it, but maybe it belongs to somebody who will lead us to Blac."

John put on his sunglasses and said, "I hope so," as they both walked to the street where their undercover car was parked. They got in and drove off.

Work hard and unwind harder. Asia was at the point of no return. Asia was ready to leave this life behind and start a new one. She lit her white candles and played her mediation music to unwind, wearing only a black silk gown and black fuzzy slippers with rollers in her hair. She was in the kitchen making one of her favorite Caribbean dishes: oxtails in gravy with coconut rice and peas, baked macaroni and cheese, cabbage and dressin'. Now, Asia was pretty good at watching her figure, but every now and then, she would dive into a feast. Besides, she had something to celebrate. She had gotten Blac off her back as far as fixing her mishaps and she had something to look forward to in the future—or did she? Asia received a FaceTime call; on the other end of the line was an emotionless Jacob. He said, "Hey," with no expression.

Asia showed her beautiful smile, smiling from ear to ear and said, "Hello, stranger." Asia was excited and the phone call couldn't have been at a more perfect time. It gave her a sense of joy and happiness.

Jacob said, "Are you home? We need to talk today."

Asia said, "I'm home. Are you hungry? I made food."

Jacob said, "No. I don't have much of an appetite these days." Asia said, "OK, well, I'm here. I'm about to drink some red wine if you want to come over.

He said, "Well, I'll be there in 10 minutes. I'm close by." Jacob drove his car to Asia's house, which wasn't hard at all, considering that for the last couple of days, he couldn't help but drive around the city collecting his thoughts and rationalizing his emotions. He knew what he saw and this was not something that he felt like he could deal with. The only way for him to know for sure was to talk to Asia, and he was going to do just that. Jacob walked into Asia's home with a serious look and carried a heavy energy with his aura. Asia leaned in for a kiss, which Jacob avoided. Confused by his reaction, Asia said, "OK... how are you?"

Jacob responded by saying, "I'm alive" Very confused

Asia said, "What does that mean?"

He said, "Asia, tell me the truth."

She said, "OK. About what?"

Jacob said, "About what you do."

She said, "What would you like to know? I believe I've told you everything that you would need to know about me."

Jacob said, "I have reason to believe you didn't. I followed you, Asia."

Asia's eyes got really big and she leaned forward, sticking

her neck out. She said, "You followed me?"

He said, "Yeah. I had been calling for a couple of days and hadn't gotten a response, so I thought I did something wrong. I felt like I should follow you because I wanted to try to see what was going on and fix whatever I did wrong because I didn't want to lose you, so I followed you. I saw you."

Asia said, "You saw me what?"

Jacob said, "I seen you coming out of that man's house and when I went inside, the man was dead in the most terrifying and horrific way I ever seen."

Asia started laughing and said, "I'm pretty sure you got out of there fast."

Jacob looked at Asia and said, "That's not funny. I could deal with you being a hoe, but I can't deal with you being a hoe *and* a killer!"

Asia said, "Well, I'm not about to babysit your emotions about it. I never lied to you."

Jacob said, "But you didn't tell me, either."

Asia said, "That is not none of your business. And as far as what you seen, that's what you get! What are you doing following me, creep? I knew you was a creep. You know what? This was a mistake."

Jacob said, "I'm thinking the same thing, considering that you don't just sleep with people, but you kill them, too."

Asia looked at him and said, "Ta-da! You figured out the riddle."

Jacob looked at Asia and said, "That's not funny."

Asia, laughing hysterically, threw her hands up and in a crazy voice said, "What are you gonna do, turn me in to the authorities?" Jacob said, "Now, you know I wouldn't do that to you. I care about you, but I can't be with you."

Asia looked at him with an annoyed and angry face and said, "What do you want me to do? Beg or cry? Definitely not doing that. I've lost way more people that were way more important to my life than you. Time heals all wounds. It was cute while it lasted, but I'm

196

fine with it. Anyways, I'm not doing this with you. You said your piece and you did what you did. Now, leave."

Jacob said, "Leave?!"

Asia said, "Am I speaking another language that you don't understand? Leave! You said your piece, you said what you needed to say, and I'm over it and I accept it, so leave."

Jacob said, "You don't have to be so rude about it. I mean, you're the one with the crazy lifestyle, not me."

Asia said, "What I'm not about to let you do is send me on a guilt trip about something that you should have already known from the beginning. Remember that *I* didn't pursue *you*—*you* pursued *me*. So, now that you know what you know, you do what you wanna do with information. And like I said, leave. And matter of fact, you have something that belongs to me? Because I'm pretty sure I left my lipstick at your house. I went to the store to get me a new one, but they're out of stock, so just give me my lipstick and then go on back to your regular, boring little saxophone life."

Jacob said, "You just crazy. You just like the people around you. I thought you were different."

Asia said, "No, I thought *you* were different. Anyways, I'm not doing this. Get my stuff."

Jacob, full of emotions and disappointment, patted his pockets in search of the lipstick that he had thought he had kept in his pocket for the last couple of days. He always intended to return the lipstick to Asia, but due to the series of events that had taken place, he wasn't able to see her and give it to her.

Jacob realized that he did not have the lipstick and said, "I don't know. Maybe I left it somewhere. Maybe I dropped it. I don't—I don't know where it's at. I did have it in my pocket, but I must have left it somewhere."

Asia said, "You left it somewhere?"

Jacob said, "Yeah. I don't know where I put it. I left it somewhere."

"Do you think it's in your house?" said Asia.

Jacob said, "I doubt it, because I put it in my pocket when I was going to meet you."

Asia said, "Wait, did you go inside the house?"

Jacob said, "How do you think I know what was going on in there?"

Asia said, "Did you leave the lipstick in the house?"

Jacob said, "I don't know. I doubt it, but I don't remember. I know that I had it before I went to meet you."

Asia feared that Jacob may have brought her more drama and trouble than she wanted.

Asia closed her eyes, shook her head and said, "You have messed up really bad."

Jacob looked at Asia with a confused look and said, "What are you talking about, 'I messed up really bad'?"

Asia said, "You have a lipstick of mine and you don't know where you left it at. All you know is that it could possibly be at the scene of a man's murder, and you don't think that's an issue?"

Jacob looked at Asia with a very scared and shocked face and said, "I—I mean, I can go look and see if I have it, but I—I don't remember."

Asia stopped him and said, "Stop stuttering. You're making me nervous. OK, just get out because I have to fix this. Get out! Get out! Get out! Get out! Get out!" as she pushed Jacob out the door. He walked backwards, trying to keep his balance, and when they got to the doorway, Asia slammed the door in his face.

Jacob shouted, "I didn't mean to! I'm sorry!"

Asia yelled through the door, "Yeah, *you're* sorry, huh? Well, *I'm* sorry I ever met you!"

Asia quickly gathered her thoughts as she got dressed and headed over to Blac's office. Asia's head was spinning with thoughts. Her fantasy was truly too good to be her reality; Jacob wasn't really ready to accept her for who she was, but that was her fault, 'cause she had told him some things that made him run from her reality. Maybe she just was who she was and this was who she would always be; maybe her relationship with Jacob really had been too good to be true. She kicked herself for letting her emotions lead her and started to question her understanding of life and the things she had been taught. She knew that feelings and letting her guard down had allowed her to believe that there could be something different out there for her and that Jacob could be the one to give it to her. That wasn't the only thing that was going through her mind; she was also worried about where he had left her lipstick. This could be detrimental to her freedom. She was disappointed in love and in herself for taking a chance because things appeared to align and make sense. She lost herself and allowed someone else to control how she thought and felt, but most all, Jacob was able to insert himself in her business life because she allowed her work life and love life to collide. She allowed herself to get emotionally caught up with a man who appeared to be different and who claimed to accept who she was, which put her in a compromising position when it came to fulfilling her job duties.

So, now, she had to face Blac. Early in the development of Jacob and Asia's relationship, Blac warned Asia about the importance of being able to have control and prioritize her different roles when it came to business and pleasure. Asia got out of her car, and while trying to keep her thoughts together, she frantically got onto the elevator. Asia quickly closed the elevator door as she fought back tears and had an instant breakdown. Everything in her resembled a hopeless little girl who had removed her guard and was shattering from the pain of her emotions. As she wiped her face and teary eyes, she realized that she was close to her destination and pulled herself together. Asia walked out of the elevator and marched up the hall to Blac's office. Angelica stopped Asia and asked her if there was something she could help her with. Asia quickly entered, displaying no emotion on her face, and walked past Angelica.

She brushed Angelica off and said, "You can't help me with anything. Where is Blac?"

Very frightened, Angelica sat in her seat, pointed to Blac's office and said, "Blac's in. You can just go in."

Now, normally, Angelica would give Asia grief about her being privileged in Blac's life and not having to follow anyone's rules other than her own. But due to Asia's demeanor and the expression on her face, Angelica knew that it was not a good time to mess with her. Asia walked into Blac's office, where Blac was sitting with some papers. A sexy, curly-headed Blac with glasses on her face lifted her head and put her right hand on her chin. She looked at Asia and said, "What happened?"

Asia closed her eyes and began to get teary eyed. Blac pushed herself away from her desk on her black velvet swivel chair and stood up.

"Don't do that. Don't do that," Blac said. She got up and locked the door. Blac was internally panicking; she was not prepared for what Asia was going to say, but she knew to get ready because she knew that this would be an intense conversation. Asia sat down on the couch in Blac's office and Blac approached her very slowly, taking in Asia's heavy emotions. Blac sat down next to Asia and intertwined her fingers with hers.

"I did everything right except for…" said Asia. Blac looked at her, pouting to show empathy. Asia said, "I guess… I guess you were right."

Blac said, "I haven't made it this far by being wrong, but what happened?"

Asia said, "Well, long story short, I may be getting indicted for this specific incident."

Blac shook her head, squinted her eyes tightly and said, "What? What do you mean, 'you may be getting indicted'? Do I need to send you out of the city?"

Asia said, "It may be too late. I don't know."

Blac said, "If you don't tell me what's going on, I can't help you."

Asia said, "Jacob followed me to the location and he actually *seen* Bruce's body."

Blac let go of Asia's hands and stood up. She looked to the corner, flared her nose and sucked her teeth. She looked at Asia and said, "Do I need to kill your boyfriend?"

Asia said, "I doubt it. He's already shook up enough. He

definitely don't want a part of you."

Blac said, "I'ma kill him."

Asia said, "No. Please. He's not going to do anything stupid." Blac said, "I know, 'cause he gon' die."

Asia said, "Please calm down."

Blac calmed down, then looked at Asia, walked towards her and sat next to her. After collecting her feelings, she grabbed Asia's arms and said, "Come here. I've never let you down since the day I met you. I'm not gonna start now."

Asia, at this point, had completely broken down. She was crying, upset that she let her guard down. This was something that she had never done before because she had always followed the teachings of those who molded her. She just didn't listen with her ears—she listened with her heart as well.

Blac spent a moment consoling Asia and letting her know that she would get through this and that there was a bigger picture to consider.

Blac looked Asia in the eyes and said, "OK. Enough of that. You'll be fine. Now, where's my $200?"

Asia looked at Blac with black mascara all over her face and said, "What?" in a cracking voice.

Blac held her hand out in front of Asia and said, "Yes, for my consoling and counseling session."

Asia said, "You're pretty steep, don't you think?"

Blac stood up and said, "Psh, no, especially considering that your tears are on my Chanel. Hell, I gotta be paid for my services just like everybody else. It would be nice to recoup some of the fees y'all been charging me all this time."

Asia said, "Ain't that about... nothing?" as she grabbed a tissue off the table and wiped her face.

Blac said, "Yes, ma'am. Clean yo'self up. Nobody has sympathy for killers and hoes, and you happen to be both."

Asia said, "Ouch."

Blac said, "Truth hurts, but pain and pressure creates beautiful diamonds. While no one said that what we do is right, somewhere in our minds, we justify it to sleep peacefully. And yes, we're the villains depending on who you ask, but we possess so many positive qualities, and for me, that's enough.

So, while you don't deserve sympathy, I can empathize with your heart still because you're human."

Asia said, "Well, thank you, Great One. But I think I got a handle on my feelings. I'll be fine."

Blac said, "Sure, you will, and don't worry. I'll take care of it. Don't worry."

Asia put her tissue in the trash and walked out of Blac's office.

Angelica came in to see a somewhat worried Blac standing in the big window of her office.

Angelica said, "Can I come in?"

Blac looked back at the door and said, "Yeah, you can come," as she walked to her desk and sat down. Angelica walked in with a cute, high-energy bop to her walk like she normally did. She sat a small stack of papers on Blac's desk and said, "I got news for you." Blac said, "I can't take no more news today," as she tried to sit up straight in her chair.

Angelica shuffled through the papers and read from documents. "Lola, is it? Well, she started in the police force with top honors. She busted up a bunch of people and put them behind bars. But her family history is kind of normal, except that her dad got killed when she was about 10. No one really knows why or how he got killed, but he seemed noble. Here is a newspaper clip of her saying she was the daughter of an award-winning doctor.

Blac became interested in what Angelica was saying and said, "You got a picture of her mom and dad?"

Angelica handed Blac the papers and said, "I guess this is her father."

Blac said, "This is Lola's father?"

Angelica said, "Yes. You know him?"

Blac looked at the picture and a cold dark energy came over the room. Blac quickly got herself together and said, "No, I don't,

202

but I'll figure out what I'm gonna do with this information because I'm sick of this girl. She's been a pain in my rear for some time now, and quite frankly, I'm tired of it."

Angelica said, "Well, OK. Is there anything else you need from me?"

Blac looked at Angelica and said, "Why don't you take the rest of the day off?"

Angelica looked at Blac and said, "You sure?"

Blac said, "I'm sure."

Angelica said, "Well, thank you," and left Blac's office in a cheery mood. While Angelica packed up with excitement, Blac was living out the understanding that if you don't deal with something, it only comes back to haunt you. No matter how it's dressed, it feels the same—even when you act like it never happened and hope that it never comes back to find you.

Blac never felt the need to lie to anyone or keep things from certain people. She was definitely open and upfront when it came to her past and the obstacles that she had to face in order to become who she was. But she wasn't the type to offer the juicy details of her life to just any listening ears, either.

Blac picked up her phone and made a phone call.

A very deep and dominant voice on the other end of the phone answered and said, "What's going on, Big Mama?"

Blac, in a very cute and innocent voice, said, "Hey, Daddy. I got a situation." She was talking to Charlie.

Charlie said, "Handle yo' business. You don't need me!"

Black smirked and said, "Yes, I do," while rolling her eyes.

Charlie said, "Really?"

Blac said, "Definitely."

Charlie said, "Oh, this must be big. What's wrong?"

Blac went into detail about what had happened between Asia and Jacob, and the fact that he possibly may have given the detectives the answer they needed in order to put Asia at the crime scene. If anybody could make all of this go away, it was Charlie. Charlie was the baby of a family who had been running the city for over a hundred years. Aired to the throne, Charlie had to hand in his pistols for cigars and learn how to get his point across in a more sensible and peaceful manner. But don't get me wrong—they got their hands dirty, too, when it was necessary. The difference was that they didn't keep their doings secret and nobody was safe.

After listening to what she said, Charlie said, "Don't worry, Mama. I do stuff like that in my sleep. I'll pull some strings and see what's going on. Don't you worry your pretty little head; I got it."

Blac, bringing back the innocent and cute voice, said,

"Thanks, Daddy. I know I can always depend on you."

"Always and forever," Charlie said. "I'll be home tonight, so I'll see you then and we can talk about it."

Blac said, "OK. I love you."

Charlie said, "I love you, too."

Blac hated doing this, but when it was necessary, it was necessary. She reached out to Charlie to get some assistance with this specific situation because she just didn't feel like dealing with it. While she probably could have done it herself, it wasn't worth the energy. Plus, it stroked her ego to know that she had the top dog on a tight leash. If she told him to jump, he would ask, "How high?" Who said you can't teach an old dog new tricks? Blac had no complaints or problems in that area, so she used it to her advantage when she needed to.

The next afternoon, Lola left a coffee shop and headed to the office to gather notes regarding Bruce's murder. At this time, Lola had received the ballistics back from the lipstick, and it belonged to Asia. Asia had a clean record and Lola did not have much information on her, but she was definitely going to bring her in for questioning because she was the only possible lead on this case. Lola didn't know if this was a woman who Bruce had an encounter with or someone who accidentally dropped their lipstick while walking through the neighborhood. But in a perfect world, this was a woman who was involved in his murder and accidentally left it on the premises. Either way, Lola was planning on bringing Asia in for questioning and she was gonna decide where she fit in the case.

As Lola put her key into the driver's side door to get into her car, a black SUV pulled up and blocked her into her parking spot. Two men got out, grabbed Lola, put her into the back of the SUV and drove off. Another black SUV drove behind the first. Lola sat in the middle of two big men while two other big men sat in front of her. All of the men were in black and she knew exactly why they were kidnapping her. One said, "Hey, Lola."

Lola looked at the man and said, "You know who I am, so you know I'm a detective. This is illegal."

The man rolled his eyes and said, "Ain't nobody scared of you.

I just need you to take this phone call."

The man picked up his phone and said, "Yeah, Boss. I got her."

The man on the other end of the phone screamed, "Let me talk to her!"

The man beside Lola handed her the phone.

In a hesitant voice, Lola said, "Hello?"

Charlie, the man on the phone said, "Lola, what are you doing?"

Lola squinted her face as if the man was screaming in her face. His voice was definitely loud.

He projected his voice even more and said, "I'm pretty sure you know *what* I am and *who* I am. Now, we can play this guessing game, but neither of us have time for that. What I *do* want to know is, why are you so concerned with this case?"

Lola said, "Newsflash: It's *my* case."

Charlie said, "Well, close it. I'm sorry, that's insensitive; you have a job to do. Well, do you know who the killer is?" Lola said, "Not yet, but we have somebody. An interest." Charlie said, "Wrong answer!!! *No*, you *don't* have an interest, because *you* control the case. You wanna be able to live and work in the city, don't you? My love, I don't make threats; things just *happen*. And I would hate to see something unfortunate happen to you due to your role in the case. So, close it."

Lola said, "I can't do that. I have a job to do."

Charlie said, "OK. You have it. Do your job and I'm gonna do mine."

She said, "Well, I guess we're just gonna have to do our jobs." Charlie stopped Lola and said, "Lola."

Lola got very quiet and didn't say much, 'cause at this point, she have had enough. She had no more words; she had no interest in closing the case. So, she thought, whatever Charlie felt like he had to do must be done.

Charlie noticed the silence on the phone and said, "Well, you don't have anything else to say and neither do I. I said what I said and what is bound to happen will happen."

Lola said, "Well, can you tell your goons to drop me off?"

Charlie said, "With pleasure."

Lola gave the phone back to the man, who said, "Alright, Boss," to Charlie. Charlie's men dropped her off at her car; she quickly got in and locked her doors. Lola was a nervous wreck. She couldn't believe what had just happened. She knew that she had little to no time to get her case moving before anything significant happened. Lola drove to the precinct and sat at her desk. John walked over to the desk to find a disturbed Lola. He touched her shoulder and she quickly turned around.

John raised his hands and said, "It's just me."

Lola turned back around and started biting her nails while going over her notes.

John sat down and said, "Hey, are you OK?"

Lola said, "No, I'm not OK. I got picked up."

John said, "Picked up? By who?"

Lola said, "I don't know. Some man wit' big goons and a big mouth."

John said, "What he look like?"

Lola said, "I didn't see him?"

John said, "Was your head covered?"

Lola got frustrated, leaned in and whispered while gritting her teeth. "All I know is, four big guys dressed in all black with masks over their faces snatched me up and put me in the car. Then, this dude got on the phone talking crazy to me."

John said, "Let's go talk to the captain."

Lola said, "And risk losing this case? Are you crazy? No. This girl is connected to Blac and I'm going to prove it."

John shook his head and said, "Blac is going to be the death of you."

Lola said, "No, she isn't. But we are about to see who the death of Bruce was."

John said, "What do we have?"

Lola said, "We have Asia. While she has no record and nothing that ties her to Blac, let's pick her up and see if she can connect some of our dots."

John said, "Let's go."

Lola and John went to pick up Asia. Lola wanted to be as discreet as possible, so she got a tip that Asia had a set grooming day and time for her dog.

As Asia walked into the shop, there were two people sitting there who appeared to be undercover cops. She didn't pay too much attention—at least, she didn't want to make it seem like she was paying them any mind. She gave her dog to the attendant that usually groomed her and left the shop. While Asia stood outside, Lola walked up to her.

She said, "Hello, ma'am. My name is Lola. I have a few questions for you."

Asia looked at Lola and said, "Am I under arrest?"

Lola said, "I would just like to ask you a couple of questions."
Asia said, "I think I need to call my lawyer."

Lola said, "Well, I tried to do it the easy way, but now I'm gonna need you to put your hands up."

Asia said, "Put my hands up?"
she said, "Yes, put your hands up. We have probable cause to bring you to the police station for questioning."

Asia said, "Regarding what?"

John said, "Mr. Bruce."

Asia didn't resist because she knew that she had done everything right, but she couldn't help but wonder what Jacob may have done for them to be bringing her in. Asia kept her composure, but her mind most certainly wandered.

When the car approached the precinct, Lola saw a man dressed in a sharp, tan suit standing in front of the building and waving at her car. Under her breath, she mumbled, "Go figure." John looked at her and said, "What?" as he parked.

Lola pointed to the man and said, "Asia, it looks like your knight in shining armor is here." As Lola walked Asia to the front door, Lola looked at the lawyer and said, "Alex, why am I not surprised?"

Alex smiled and said, "Hello to you, too."

Lola said, "Alex, what are you doing here?"

Alex said, "Shouldn't I be asking *you* what *you're* doing and if you have a warrant for her arrest?"

Lola said, "She possibly has some information about a murder, so we're just bringing her in for questioning."

Alex said, "Absolutely. I don't mind sitting in. I'm a watcher, anyways."

Lola rolled her eyes.

They walked into the precinct, and as he wished, Alex sat in on the interrogation regarding Bruce's murder. Lola, annoyed by Alex's presence, asked a stream of basic questions. After a short period, Alex interjected.

Alex said, "Do you have anything that puts her in the house?" Lola screwed up her face at Alex and said, "Asia, when was the last time you saw this lipstick?"

Asia said, "About two weeks ago."

Lola said, "Where did you lose it?"

Asia said, "I'm not sure. It must have fell out my purse."

Lola said, "Do you know Bruce?"

Asia said, "No."

Alex said, "Don't answer anything else, Asia. Lola, this is a waste of my time and yours and you know it. Book her or let her go."

The district attorney, standing in a small room and wearing a black pantsuit with her black curly hair in a top bun, knocked on the glass.

Lola walked into the small room and shut the door.

The district attorney said, "Let her go."

Lola said, "What?"

The district attorney said, "Sorry. We don't have any reason to hold her. Give me something I can work with and I'll haul her back in."

Lola walked back into the interrogation room, where she delivered the news that Asia was able to go home. "Well, Miss Asia, we appreciate your time regarding Bruce's murder. If there is any way that you can help or if you know a person who can help us, please let us know."

Asia's lawyer laughed and said, "So you couldn't hold her?" Lola looked at him, rolled her eyes and said, "Not just yet, since you wanna talk."

He said, "Are you saying she's a suspect? Now you're talking to me like she's a suspect."

Lola looked at him and said, "I know you're a crooked lawyer. You deal with crooked people, so the fact that she has you for a lawyer makes her guilty already."

He looked at Lola as he closed his suit jacket and said, "Oooooh! Talk to me dirty. Well, until you can get something that sticks to my client, please leave us alone. Do not seek my client anymore unless you have something that puts her on the *inside* of the crime scene and not just on the outside, please."

Lola looked at him and said, "You know, you are the scum of the system."

The lawyer looked Lola in her eyes and said, "But I don't kiss and tell."

John tapped Lola and said, "Hey, you got a phone call and it's urgent."

Lola looked at her partner, looked back at Alex and said,

"We'll see you soon." Lola walked through the busy precinct to her desk.

Lola said, "This is Lola."

A woman's scratchy voice delivered bad news through the phone. Lola instantly dropped the phone. She felt like somebody had sucked the breath from her body. She was hoping that she was in the middle of a sick dream and that she would wake up at any moment. Lola grabbed her things, barely feeling the things she touched; her body seemed to have gone numb. The only thing that was registering in her mind was that Scarlett was dead. Sorrow overflowing, she walked out to her car. Asia and her lawyer were outside of the precinct getting into a limousine with black tinted windows. On the driver's side in the back was Blac. She rolled her window, stuck her head out of the window and blew Lola a kiss before rolling her window back up.

Lola quickly got in her car and drove off as she kept looking at her rearview mirrors to make sure she wasn't being followed. Lola replayed the phone call in her mind over and over again. A voice said, "Scarlett is dead. Somebody shot her in a drive-by shooting. Every time Lola heard those words in her head, her heart broke more and more. Lola felt like someone had opened up her body and was pouring acid on her organs. This was the highest level of pain a person could endure. Not only did she feel pain; she also felt responsibility and guilt. Lola knew that her beloved had been killed as a result of her job and her desire to enter into the city's underworld. Lola cried and sobbed as she had flashbacks of the woman that she would no longer be able to love or touch ever again.

CHAPTER 16
SWALK AWAY WITH A STRUT

As the driver dropped Alex to his car, Blac thanked him for his services and expressed her gratitude for his availability. Alex accepted her nice words and went about his day. Asia looked at Blac and said, "I'm done."

Blac said, "It's about time."

Asia looked at Blac with a shocked face and said, "You don't seem surprised."

Blac said, "I'm grateful! But no, I'm not. I figured this would be the end of it for you, because when it gets this hectic and everything's against you and you can't control it, it's time to walk away. Asia, you got a chance. Take it before it's too late."

Asia said, "Blac, it's not too late for you, either."

Blac said, "A lot of things about my life you don't know because it's not for you to know. But there's a reason why everything that's happening is happening, and it would be selfish of me to act like I didn't see it coming and derail you. I wouldn't be able to allow you to continue on this path knowing that I could possibly put you in a position where I can't protect you. So, I'm happy you're done, because I'm done for you."

Asia, very relieved, leaned back and looked out the window at her house as Blac granted her blessing to leave the underworld life. Asia had learned and conquered what she felt like she needed to in that world; once you reach a certain level of knowledge and recognize that you're bigger than what's around you, it's time to get out. Fortunately for Asia, she had someone who was rooting for her. Blac gave Asia a bag of money with $50 million in it and said, "Not that I think you need it, but this is something that'll get you through.

This is a parting gift and I never want to see you again."

Asia said, "I got the idea." They laughed, hugged and held each other tightly for a moment.

This was the end of a chapter and the beginning of a new one for Asia. Blac sat and watched her walk into the house like a proud mom sending her child off to her first day of school. She accepted the fact that their relationship was built on more than just business and found peace in knowing that she was able to grant Asia the blessing of leaving her life in the underworld behind and not ending up behind bars or in a casket.

CHAPTER 17
THE TAKEOVER

The next day, Asia felt a sense of bittersweet relief. She was happy to close a very active and knowledgeable chapter of her life. She slept through most of her morning while deciphering her goals and plans. While going through her thoughts, she couldn't help but think about Jacob. Asia envisioned everything about him, from his smile to how he touched her and how he made her feel. She could honestly say that she was very much in like, and maybe in love, with this man. Asia had a lot of gratitude for him because he opened her eyes in ways that nobody else could. Due to her newfound love for him, she was willing to quit all of her ways in order to build a future with him. She was really done; she walked away from life in the underworld and hoped that he would be willing to continue a future with her. But she had one more thing to do before she started her quest to a new life.

Asia got dressed in a navy blue cocktail dress and nude shoes. As always, she draped her neck in pearls and wore her diamond stud earrings. Asia walked into The Black Silhouette. The place had a different feel to it during the day. There was no loud band with a beautiful lead songstress singing the soundtrack of the night, just a pianist who played smooth melodies to the nearly empty room. "There you are, pretty," said the older Black gentleman who had been bartending at the spot since Blac first brought her there.

Asia smiled, sat at the bar and said, "If I can't guarantee anybody else to be here, I know you always will be."

The gentleman looked at Asia and said, "When it's not a soul in sight! Same as usual?

Asia smiled and said, "Yup," as the bartender handed her a

small glass with three ice cubes and a double shot of cognac in it.

She looked at him and said, "How do you survive in this chaos?"

The man put the towel on the bar and said, "I hear the whispers, but I learn to take the good with the bad because I stand on morals and consequences. They go hand in hand. But most of all, I do it for people like you."

Asia perked up and said, "Me?"

He said, "Yes, you... the ones who need a safe place where only the ones like them can relate"

Asia said, "Well, I'm done."

He said, "And that's why I do it—to see the chosen ones."

Asia said, "What do you mean?"

He said, "The ones who know when to walk away." Asia smiled, kissed him on the forehead and said, "Goodbye, good guy."

The man said, "Forever, little lady."

Asia walked out, leaving The Black Silhouette the common location of a once beautiful horror story. She walked until she was in the middle of the parking lot, then turned and looked back as flashbacks of her happiest times to her darkest hours came across her brain. This was the end and she was happy to see it. While she stood there, a voice crept up behind her and said, "Going somewhere?"

Asia quickly turned around to find Jacob breathing down her neck. She smiled and said, "How did you know?"

Jacob said, "A sweet little birdie told me. Reached out to me and broke the news."

Asia smiled and said, "Blac?"

Jacob said, "I have something to say. You are wonderful. You are smart. You are worthy of being loved and worshipped as a queen. I am *so* sorry for not understanding every part of who you are. After talking to Blac, I realized that I don't want to die alone. I want to live and build with you."

Asia said, "My turn. I can't imagine life without you. You opened my eyes in ways I didn't think was possible. So, I choose you."

Jacob said, "I choose you. I love you."

Asia said, "Let's leave."

Jacob said, "And go where?"

Asia said, "I don't know. Let's move to Miami! I wanna start fresh."

Jacob said, "Oh, how I've missed you."

Their faces touched as they fell into a passionate and soul tying kiss.

Asia and Jacob went away to start a new life in Florida. This was a beautiful thing; they were starting a new life together while Lola was making amends and picking up hers.

Lola took personal time off from work to deal with the death of her girlfriend. Lola didn't know how to fix it, but she hoped that her remorse was felt through her presence. She sat with her knees in the grass of the cemetery that housed the body of her once-lover as emotions came over her body and mind. Lola left a very sweet message on her headstone, along with yellow roses, which were Scarlett's favorite. As she stood up and got ready to leave, she saw a dark shadow looming over her body. Lola reached for her pistol; *Don't do it*, her inner voice told her.

Lola closed her eyes and said, "What are you doing here? Haven't you done enough?"

Blac, standing there with her hair curled and wearing an all black fur coat that went down to her ankles, looked at Lola and said, "I'm here to offer you some peace." Lola stood up, turned around and looked at Blac.

Lola said, "You have some nerve to offer me peace after everything you've done."

Blac looked at Lola and said, "Everything I've done? I've always been on the reacting side of everything."

Lola looked at Blac and said, "Have you? 'Cause Scarlett's dead."

Blac looked at Lola and said, "*You* killed Scarlett, not me. I don't even know how Scarlett got killed. Lola said, "Whatever. What do you want?"

Blac said, "Leave my people alone."

Lola said, "Not this again."

Blac said "Yes, *this* again. And this time, I'm coming with something that you might want to see." She handed Lola a manila folder. Lola opened the folder, took one look and put the papers back into the folder. She looked up at Blac and Blac raised her brow.

In a sneaky voice, Blac said, "See? I'm not the only one with dirty little secrets. You ain't as much of an angel as people think you are either and I'm pretty sure the police force would *love* to have that information."

Lola looked at Blac and said, "What else do you want from me?"

Blac said, "I just want you to leave my people alone."

Lola said, "You know what you are and I don't need to do anything to you. You will kill yourself eventually. You may have won this battle, but remember, I'ma win this war."

Blac looked at Lola and said, "I doubt it, but whatever you need to tell yourself to sleep at night." She walked away, leaving Lola at her dead lover's headstone holding the one thing that could shatter her entire world.

LETTER TO THE READER

First, I would like to say thank you. This is my first published piece of literature and you, for whatever reason, decided to support me, and for that alone I am grateful. If you get to this page that means one of two things happened, you read the whole book which would make me very happy or you skipped to this part so you can know what I want you to take away from this story to decide if you're gonna read the whole book.

So, what did I want you to take away from this story? Did I want you to take away from the story that it's okay to kill people if you have a reason? Did I want you to say or think it's okay to be involved or around prostitute rings long as no one is forcing you to?

The answer is no to all, the story doesn't glorify, nor does it promote any type of illegal activities. What it does is gives you understanding and education through relatable and understanding events and scenarios, so you learn the valuable hidden messages like thinking things through and being able to consciously make a smart decision that does not put you or anybody around you in harm's way. If I can give you just one lesson in this whole story it's to always think things through; never make decisions off impulse or emotions too many times we as people make impulsive and irrational decisions and they are justified by being dressed up as "gangster" or "real" when the reality is more often than not, the decision is usually premature and stupid. The reason why the ladies were so powerful and roofless in this story was that they presented something in front of your face that the victims couldn't see past. While they may have disrespected these ladies, especially Blac, they didn't realize that sometimes the power is not seen and the one who you don't expect to be a threat is the biggest threat. Out of my 30 years of living, I've seen it happen so many times. I've seen so many people put so much into other people who they feel aren't threats or couldn't understand what's going on around them, when the reality is some of the people who you believe aren't threats are some of the biggest threats to you. They are strategic and patient when it comes time to victimize, so don't allow the arrogance or ignorance of your thoughts, what you see on TV or social media make you a victim.

Again, thank you for reading this book. I hope you were entertained as well as educated and I hope to see you in Part 2 where we learn another lesson about not thinking with our heads and thinking with our eyes.

Made in the USA
Middletown, DE
28 October 2022

13572438R00124